THE
GARDENER'S
ALMANAC

THE GARDENER'S ALMANAC

FEATURING

TIPS, TRUTHS and FORECASTS for the URBAN, SUBURBAN and COUNTRY GARDENER

Edited by
Peter C. Jones & Lisa MacDonald

Designed by Doris Straus

HOUGHTON MIFFLIN COMPANY
Boston   New York

Designed by Doris Straus

A High Tide Press book.

For information about permission to reproduce selections from this book, write to:
Permissions, Houghton Mifflin Company, 215 Park Avenue South, New York,
New York 10003.

For information about this and other Houghton Mifflin trade and reference books
and multimedia products, visit The Bookstore at Houghton Mifflin on the World
Wide Web at http://www.hmco.com/trade/.

CIP data is available.

ISBN 0-395-82755-8

Printed in the United States of America

QUM 10 9 8 7 6 5 4 3

TABLE OF CONTENTS

IX THE LEARNED GARDENER

X THE GREEN GARDENER

XI GARDENING ON THE NET

My First Garden

by Thomas C. Cooper

Gardens surrounded me from my earliest days, but I am not one of those who took to growing primulas at age two and never looked back. My first real garden, in fact, was a long time coming. We lived in southern Vermont, which was thoroughly rural in those days, and the surrounding mountains and meadows were filled with plants. I was introduced to many plants and learned much about their habits and moods, though there was nothing cultivated about them. Still, it was the beginning of a gardening education that I draw on to this day.

In spring skunk cabbage grew in swarms along the riversides; in summer goldenrod shimmered while birches brought a sense of cool and quiet; in fall asters billowed among the roadside grasses; and in winter stone walls and trees stood stark against mountains of snow. I early got to know the Jack-in-the-pulpits that grew in the boggy ground at the northeastern corner of the Meachams' field, the moose maple that formed clumps along the Mettawee River (and that made excellent carving sticks), the mauve phlox surrounding Chappy Chapman's rusted and deserted hand water pump, the sugar maples whose sap we collected in midwinter and whose leaves we raked and burned in autumn.

The first formal garden I knew was the one that surrounded our house. It was a loose collection of shrubs and herbaceous beds, vegetable and fruit plots. Many of the plants my parents had inherited from the previous owner, and they bore the stamp of her Victorian upbringing: hydrangeas, columbines, ferns, phlox, and stiff conifers. Though I absorbed these sights without any thought of becoming a gardener, the lessons of gardening seep into one, just as the love of it does. So I learned the virtues of digging a proper hole with straight walls and preparing the soil thoroughly before planting. The virtues (and pleasures) of record keeping struck me then, as did the need to string pea wire tightly, to make bean poles tall enough, and to stockpile manure.

None of this information came rushing out when I undertook to make my own first garden in a rumpled and tired little field near the coast north of Boston. I spent weeks happily wrestling a rented tiller over the slightly sloping ground. I planted standard things: 'Black Seeded Simpson' lettuce and 'Big Boy' tomatoes, cucumbers, beans, radishes, pumpkins, and 'Sugar and Butter' corn.

I also had schemes for an ornamental bed running along one side of the drive. I had, however, unfortunately missed the fundamental lesson—well known to my father and Jim Crockett, whose books I lugged everywhere—that beds are best readied in the fall, so the winter can knead the soil and the gardener can go right to work in spring. By the time I'd gotten the vegetable garden under way, there was little left of spring. Hastily I turned over the soil, gave it a slight blessing of manure, and tucked in the plants.

Through the early summer they put on a brave show, but the heat of summer sapped their puny reserves of energy and they faltered. Mildew coated the monarda, the geraniums suffered an attack of ennui. Even the daylilies were listless and straggly. Most died by the end of summer. Down the hill, the vegetables were growing well, but they had been discovered by woodchucks and beetles and other scourges. I am a little surprised it was not my last garden.

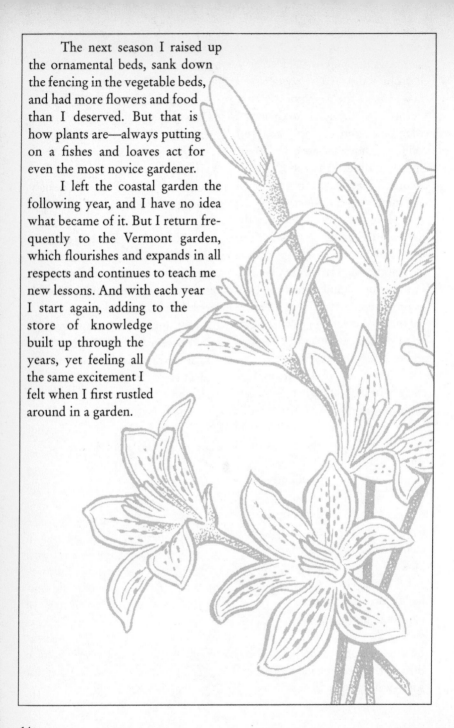

The next season I raised up the ornamental beds, sank down the fencing in the vegetable beds, and had more flowers and food than I deserved. But that is how plants are—always putting on a fishes and loaves act for even the most novice gardener.

I left the coastal garden the following year, and I have no idea what became of it. But I return frequently to the Vermont garden, which flourishes and expands in all respects and continues to teach me new lessons. And with each year I start again, adding to the store of knowledge built up through the years, yet feeling all the same excitement I felt when I first rustled around in a garden.

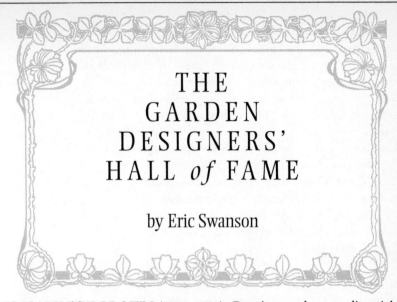

THE GARDEN DESIGNERS' HALL *of* FAME

by Eric Swanson

"CAPABILITY" BROWN (1715–1783) Despite a rather peculiar nickname, this bold British landscape designer was not a woman. Lancelot Brown earned his sobriquet through constantly referring to garden sites as having "capabilities of improvement." Abandoning the rigidly symmetrical designs of his predecessors, Brown popularized a softer, more naturalistic look. He removed fences and walls that traditionally separated estate gardens from the woodlands surrounding them, creating a more expansive vista of undulating meadows planted with clumps of trees and dotted with lakes, rivers, and ponds. He also banished most of the stone cherubs and naked goddesses associated with formal garden design, replacing them with rather nice-smelling shrubbery.

THOMAS CHURCH (1902–1978) Church began practicing in California, where increasing numbers of American families occupied homes situated on hillsides and other irregular tracts. He planned innovative gardens for these modern cliff dwellers, using raised beds, wide timber decks, broadly paved areas, and asymmetrical plots to create a sense of greater space than actually existed. He pioneered the idea of the garden as an outdoor room, where people might work, entertain, or sunbathe. Church was also one of the first landscape architects to use concrete to distinguish separate areas of the garden and is credited with designing the first kidney-shaped pool.

ANDREW JACKSON DOWNING (1815–1852) Downing adapted the romantic ideas of English designers into two distinct approaches: the "beautiful," which featured rolling hills of turf broken by groups of bushy trees or clumps of willows, and the "picturesque," characterized by wild woods, wild meadows, and streams rushing wildly among wild ferns and lichens. A prolific author and editor of a widely read horticultural journal, Downing quickly became America's leading authority on landscape design; in 1851 he was chosen to design the grounds of the Capitol, the White House, and the Smithsonian Institution. Unfortunately, a tragic steamboat accident prevented him from overseeing their completion, which was carried out by his associate, Calvert Vaux.

BEATRIX FARRAND (1872–1959) Farrand's genius lay in her ability to preserve the natural features of a landscape while complementing the existing architecture of the home. She used the dramatic contours of Dumbarton Oaks of the Robert Bliss estate in Washington, D.C., for example, to create a series of sunken outdoor "rooms" and elevated terraces. In England, she cleared away centuries of improvements to Dartington Hall, uncovering many of the landscape's original features and augmenting their individuality with careful planting of homogenous flowering shrubs and climbing wall plants. Though she preferred to be called a "landscape gardener," Farrand was nonetheless appointed the first female member of the American Society of Landscape Architects.

GERTRUDE JEKYLL (1843–1932) When severe myopia forced Jekyll to abandon her original aspiration to become a painter, she turned her prodigious talent to the art of gardening. Her most significant contribution to the field was in the deployment of color. On the grounds of English country homes designed by her longtime friend Edwin Lutyens, Jekyll demonstrated that no color stands alone but distinguishes itself only in relation to the colors around it. The chaotic palette typical of English cottage gardens became the grand passion of her life, as attested in the 13 books she wrote on the subject of gardening and more vividly in some 300 gardens she designed.

SIR GEOFFREY JELLICOE (1900–1996) A career spanning more than five decades has confirmed Jellicoe as the foremost British landscape designer of the 20th century. Naturally, such longevity has involved a certain flexibility of approach, and one of the hallmarks of Jellicoe's style has been his ability to fuse classical and modern themes. His first major commission was an English adaptation of an Italian Renaissance garden, while one of his most important later designs was a modern allegory of the stages of human life. Jellicoe's designs range in scale from big to enormous. He has landscaped entire towns, devised innovative solutions to the problems of land reclamation at several quarry operations, and most recently designed a theme park in Texas.

JENS JENSEN (1860–1951) Jensen emigrated from Denmark to the United States in 1884, settling in Chicago in 1886. He held several public park positions until 1920, when the machinations of Chicago politics inspired his early retirement. Thereafter he worked for private clients. Along with Thomas Church, Jensen was one of the first landscape architects in the United States to promote the use of regional materials. His creative arrangements of prairie grasses and other midwestern plant material to dramatize the somewhat dry local climate and generally level landscape, rather than compensate or apologize for it, came to be described as the "Prairie Style."

ANDRÉ LE NÔTRE (1613–1700) Several generations of the Le Nôtre family devoted their horticultural expertise to the estates of France's ruling class. Grandfather Pierre was appointed one of the chief gardeners of the Tuileries under Catherine de Médicis. He was succeeded in this position by his son, Jean, who also designed several other royal gardens for Louis XIII. But the unquestioned star of the family was Jean's son, André. The vast, magnificently stylized gardens he designed for Louis XIV and other French nobles made him the most celebrated landscape architect of his time, and his work inspired designers for years after his death. At the Tuileries, he cleared the land around the castle to show off its architectural splendor, while complementing its formal details through an ingenious arrangement of grottoes, terraces, compartmentalized flower beds, and sculpted shrubbery. The gardens he created at Versailles, meanwhile, still astound visitors with their sheer complexity and scale. Yet even though Le Nôtre designed on a grand scale, he never lost sight of the whole in planning the particular: balance and harmony remain the hallmarks of his style. Although Versailles is probably his most famous work, many people consider his design for Vaux-le-Vicomte, with its subtle interplay of levels and perspective, to be his most beautiful.

FREDERICK LAW OLMSTED (1822–1903) The "father of American landscape architecture" decided on his career after a chance meeting with Andrew Jackson Downing. A subsequent tour of England awakened him to the appalling lack of public parks in the United States, and in 1857 he secured a job in New York City overseeing 840 acres of swamp, rock, and immigrant shanties known as Central Park. In 1858, together with Downing's former partner, Calvert Vaux, Olmsted won city approval to improve the park grounds. Adapting Downing's "picturesque" approach to the needs of a major urban center, he sank a series of roads beneath the park, which allowed commercial vehicles to move freely across town without disturbing pedestrian or equestrian traffic. His work is reflected in more than 80 public parks across the country.

RUSSELL PAGE (1906–1985) Though his great love for plants ultimately inspired him to take up the trowel, Page initially left England to study painting in France, where proximity to the Mediterranean gave him a lasting appreciation for the interplay of light and water. Like Gertrude Jekyll, Page brought an impressive knowledge of color to the field of garden design, but he preferred classical French simplicity over rural English profusion, and he earnestly shunned any tendency toward "exuberance." At Longleat, Wiltshire, he replaced elaborate flower beds planted at the height of the Victorian era with less intricate, single-color arrangements and cleared away many of the exotic additions to the wide, rambling park originally designed by "Capability" Brown. Very late in his career, he designed the grounds of the Pepsico offices in upstate New York, where his expertise in the use of light and water as design elements brilliantly showcased a collection of modern sculpture.

WILLIAM ROBINSON (1838–1935) Robinson began his career in Ireland but moved to London in 1861 to join the staff of the Royal Botanic Gardens in Regent's Park. His profound understanding of the growth cycles of both native and imported plants ultimately revolutionized the art of gardening in England. In a number of books and articles, Robinson dispelled the widely held notion that imported species could not be successfully grown outdoors, and he encouraged his contemporaries to abandon formally arranged beds in favor of a mixed array of local and hardy exotic species. His emphasis on informality and subtle combinations of color shaped many of the ideas later made popular by his close friend Gertrude

Jekyll, and their combined influence can be seen in many gardens today.

VITA SACKVILLE-WEST (1892–1962) Celebrated in her lifetime for her fiction and poetry, and condemned for her scandalous associations with other women, Vita Sackville-West earned the permanent affection of her countrymen for the gardens she created at Sissinghurst Castle, Kent. Together with her husband, Harold Nicholson, Sackville-West transformed a weed-filled, dilapidated ruin that dated back to the Elizabethan era into what many people believe to be the quintessential English garden. While Nicholson laid out the basic plan for the gardens, Sackville-West brought together her love of history and a nostalgic yearning for the English countryside to create a romantic "tumble" of old-fashioned roses, honeysuckle, figs, and vines. Soothing colors and soft scents, and a subtle arrangement of gardens within gardens, combine to create a luxurious and restful atmosphere, enjoyed by the public since 1968, when the castle and

CHRISTOPHER COMES CALLING

BY BARBARA ASHMUN

I woke up at the crack of dawn after a restless night. Christopher Lloyd, the noted English garden writer, had arrived in Portland as a keynote speaker for the Hardy Plant Society of Oregon and was due to visit my garden. I owned all of his books and had them stacked up on the table for his autograph.

"Why on earth did I agree to have him visit?!" I asked myself. "There's nothing in my garden but forget-me-nots and feverfew, foxgloves and Jupiter's beard. And weeds!"

I'd been to see his perfect garden, centuries old with mossy stone walls, elegant slate paths, and wedding-cake staircases. Even the plants that dared seed themselves into the paving crevices were connoisseur specimens, choice cultivars of campanula and verbascum. Young muscular gardeners were everywhere—up on high ladders clipping the ancient yew hedges, down on their knees weeding the beds and borders.

I'd been tidying up my garden for weeks, but the weather had been terrible. Continuous Pacific Northwest "liquid sunshine" had produced huge weeds and enormous slugs. Serious rain had pelted the perennials, leaving them sprawled about with gaps in their centers as if an animal had sat down right in the middle.

I saw all the weaknesses in my garden and sighed. Just then I heard the sound of a car crunching down the gravel drive and realized that company had arrived. I took a deep breath and rearranged my face.

Christopher Lloyd stepped briskly out of the car. A tall, ruddy man with a full head of wavy white hair, he wore brown tweeds and an air of authority.

I greeted him warmly, and soon we were walking down the path to view the garden.

Most guests entering my garden give a flattering gasp when they catch their first glimpse of riotous color, but this time there was an ominous silence. Lloyd stopped in front of 'Russell's Cottage Rose', a fragrant pinkish purple rambler that was waving its arching canes around in search of support.

"I hate the habit of that plant," he declared.

"Well, the rain hasn't helped," I apologized.

"Oh yes, and if the sun were out, it would be the sun's fault," he shot back.

"Well, I plan to build a little summerhouse here to give the rose a place to climb and visitors a place to sit. Next year, as soon as I can take out that old apricot tree that never bears fruit."

"What do you need a summerhouse for, when you have a perfectly good house that you live in right over there? Why don't you train that rose up the apricot tree? At least it has character."

Because I hate that ugly tree, I thought to myself, smiling at the unwanted advice.

"Do you have problems with mildew and black spot on your roses?" I asked, hoping to divert him from further critiques.

"I did, but I pulled them all out. I'm growing cannas and yuccas instead."

I shuddered at the thought of replacing fragrant, colorful roses with spears of maroon and gray leaves. But what did I know, after all--I'm just an ordinary gardener who loves my flowers, trying to make the best of two-thirds of an acre of clay soil.

We advanced farther into the garden, stopping to look at a long border of Michaelmas daisies and sneezeweeds that turn into an ocean of lavender, pink, and yellow flowers every fall. Just the week before I had carefully planted a dozen annual sunflowers in this bed to jazz it up with summer color and bold foliage. The new plants were still small, waiting for some sun to help them grow. I could barely see their leaves peeking out between the neighboring perennials.

"You need stronger leaves in this planting," Lloyd declared, "better structure. And everything needs a good feed. These plants are too small."

I nodded sagely, veiling my irritation.

He marched forward toward the big summer borders.

"What a splendid patch of yellow iris over there!" he enthused. I smiled, warmed by these first words of praise. "But you've got only the one patch. You need to repeat it, perhaps another splash of yellow over there, and in that corner—a mullein, or some other plant with good leaves and vertical form."

I hated to admit that bright yellow is my least favorite color, and that the patch of yellow iris was an accident, a mistake, actually. It's such a domineering color, like a traffic sign.

"Have you thought of growing *Crambe cordifolia* in this garden?" Christopher queried. "It's quite a lovely plant with big bold leaves."

"Maybe next year," I offered. "Perhaps with some *Geranium psilostemon* nearby, and some yuccas."

"Yes, now you're getting it!" Christopher exclaimed. I smiled shyly.

"And some cannas over here? With a few bright yellow mulleins for vertical emphasis?"

"Yes, yes, that's the idea," he agreed. "But I should certainly get rid of this rose first. It's quite terrible. Look how the flowers fade so quickly."

Lloyd was pointing at 'Red Coat', one of my favorite shrub roses. It blooms from Memorial Day to Thanksgiving, with big single red flowers that I can see all the way from my bedroom window. Until now I'd never noticed just how dingy the older flowers become.

"You'll have me digging up my entire garden before this day is over!" I complained.

"Well, yes, one should always be changing," said Christopher, heading for the next bed. "Why, I had my head gardener dig out all my roses just a few months ago."

I held my tongue and counted to ten. I had no head gardener—not even an assistant gardener.

"And look over here," he went on. "You need some bolder leaves for contrast, some hostas for example. And why don't you have any ferns in the garden? And for goodness sakes, where are your hydrangeas?"

Totally deflated, I realized with relief that we'd finished our tour of the garden.

"You must come and see me again in England" were Christopher's last words to me, as he autographed the pile of his books that I'd stacked up on the picnic table.

It took me days to get over the shock of having my garden assaulted. It was like showing baby pictures only to be told that your precious child has big ears and funny hair.

My visitor was right in theory. Yes, there are standards for excellence in garden design, and it is important to have repetition, structure, and contrast. But I love my garden with all its shortcomings. With limited time and money it'll never be perfect, but it brings me oceans of joy.

I've added some bold-leaved rodgersias and castor beans, and I must admit they do improve the borders. But I love 'Red Coat' even if the flowers fade, so it's staying. As for the summerhouse, I continue to dream about it. And I still wince at bright yellow. No celebrity on earth is going to talk me into more of it!

On Collecting

by Page Dickey

I have been reading Wilfrid Blunt and laughing with pleasure. Not his classic history, *The Art of Botanical Illustration*, but a little-known book he wrote in 1963 called *Of Flowers & A Village*, in which he gleefully spoofs botanists and plants-men. The plantsman's idea of a garden, he writes, is quite different from a flower lover's: "[He] must have plants that are uncommon and difficult. . . . If a plant is blue, [he] won't rest until he's got hold of the rare albino form. . . . If it's large, he wants it small; if small, then of course he must have it enormous." And "he has a horror of all that flowers freely. . . . "

By Wilfrid Blunt's definition I would prefer to be known as a flower lover rather than a plantsman. But like many gardeners I suffer from a strong urge to collect. It must have all started with that cardboard shoe-box of trading cards when I was an unwashed nine-year-old in bushy pig-tails. (How I coveted the playing cards with a mare and foal on the front, or tumbling puppies, or the pinup pose of a movie star—could it have been Marilyn Monroe?) The fact is, I'm not above collecting all sorts of things: shoes in different colors, odd patterns of crockery, books—oh, how I love to collect books! Even chickens in a wondrous variety. I have whiled away hours pouring over the Murray McMurray Hatchery catalog— almost as interesting as any seed catalog—plotting my order of hens and roosters for spring shipment.

I certainly crave hard-to-find varieties of my favorite plants: scented pinks from England, small species of daffodils, unfamiliar snowdrops. And I've been known to covet the oddly colored flower (the white lung-wort, the near-white daylily, the yellow violet, the black cosmos, the striped zinnia). But, on the whole, I think it's fair to say that I am less a plantsman than a lover of flowers, particularly old-fashioned familiar ones; and perhaps, in my interest, more an artist than a botanist, for I like best to paint pictures with flowers and foliage. Given the choice of one rare narcissus or a hillside of daffodils, one unusual snowdrop or acres of the ordinary *Galanthus nivalis*, I would choose the hillside of daffodils, the acre of snowdrops every time.

THE ONION BRAIDER

BY ROGER B. SWAIN

He likes braiding onions. He likes braiding tight, adding in an onion every second or third plait, putting as many of the flat yellowish brown bulbs on each string as he can. Dumping the onions into a mesh sack and hanging the sack by its drawstring would keep them just as well, but these onions deserve to be done up fancy. They are his onions, and as he touches them, he remembers the times he brought them water, carefully unrolling the hose so as not to drag it over the neighboring lettuce. June and July were dry, so dry that the lilacs wilted, and water was as scarce as it was needed. To get the most out of what water was left, he scraped up a low dike of soil along the downhill side of the onion row so that the narrow stream of water flowing from the hose end stayed close to the bases of the young plants and soaked in.

Judging from the size of his onions, they had enough of everything—enough sunlight and enough fertilizer as well as water. And all of these were provided so that individual onions never had to fight to get what they needed. Over and over during the summer, he stopped and stooped to pull out even the smallest weed from the row, careful not to knock over the delicate blue-green tubular leaves of the onions themselves. There was plenty of space for weeds to grow, for he spaced the onions a full hand's breadth apart, but he tolerated no interference from volunteer seedlings of any kind. "To grow competition onions," he liked to say, "you have to grow them without competition."

Three weeks ago, with summer cooling down and the first swamp maples beginning to color, he went down the onion row with a broom, knocking over the few remaining tops that had not fallen already. And the day before yesterday he went down the row again, pulling the onions up, laying them on top of the soil with their tops all in one direction, looking as though they had been combed out by the receding tide.

Now the tops are a mix of green and brown, brown enough to be pliable, green enough to be strong. If he waited longer, the tops would become so brittle as to be unbraidable. Even now, he weaves in a length of baling twine, passing it from hand to hand along with the strands of onion tops. These onions don't need reinforcement, but using the twine had become a custom of his, partly because it is easy to tie the sisal into a loop for hanging the braid up when it is done.

He likes braiding onions. Sitting cross-legged on the cooling ground surrounded by this year's harvest, he remembers a girl's hair he braided once—long, shiny, brown hair, smelling warmly of shampoo. Most of the women he has known since have had short hair, the length of fashion and convenience. His wife's hair, though she leaves it uncut, has never grown long enough to braid properly, and all his children are sons.

Braiding onions has become an autumn ritual of his, something he fancies he is pretty good at. Of course, he would be the first to admit that there are probably onion braiders who are better. In England, perhaps. He has heard that in England there are people who double-dig their gardens every spring and spend their lives trying to grow a parsnip as big as a man's leg or the best leek in all of Lower Bottomly on the Marsh.

In the years just after he began growing vegetables, he got caught up in a bit of this sort of competition. For several seasons he grew everything in the catalog—dozens of different tomatoes, and nearly as many cucumbers, lettuces, and winter squash—entering the best of each kind in contests held at various county fairs in the state. Somewhere he still had a shoebox full of ribbons, proof that he had been pretty good at both growing and showing, but if the truth be known, the competition wasn't so stiff that the prizes meant much.

Since then, his gardening has become simpler. This year, he planted only four different tomatoes, two cucumbers, and a single squash. He no longer tries to have peas by the Fourth of July or a second crop of lettuce in the fall. He has stopped dragging hundreds of pounds of old wooden storm windows out to the garden each spring to build glass pup tents over the tomatoes, for, as he says, "open a quart of stewed tomatoes in February and who cares whether they ripened in July or September."

The only onion he still grows is called Stuttgarter. He grows them from sets, not seeds. The sets are dime-size bulbs grown the previous year by companies that sow the seed late in the season. The long days of summer cause the plants to form bulbs before the plants have had much chance to grow. Stored over the winter, these onion sets can be replanted in the spring and will resume growing, ultimately producing a full-size onion. He gets his Stuttgarter onion sets from the hardware store, 2 pounds of them every spring, roughly 400 individual sets.

Onion sets, he has found, have the virtue of yielding an onion for every one planted. And they do so consistently, even in his garden's abbreviated growing season. Full-grown Stuttgarter onions are fist-size, not as big as White Sweet Spanish onions or as colorful as Red Hamburger onions, but he has found they keep better. By hanging the braids of onions from an old hat stand on the landing of an unheated back stairway, he can count on having onions year-round. What the Stuttgarter onions lack in size they make up for in authoritativeness. A single bulb is all the pungency one wants.

He may no longer grow as many vegetables as he once did, but at least he still gardens, he reminds himself occasionally. So many of his men friends have put their gardens back to lawn. Some decided they preferred golf. Others, once they had grown everything once, moved on to new frontiers. Some gave up when they realized that unless they stored away part of the harvest, a vegetable garden fed the family for only ten weeks a year. Others quit when they stopped and calculated how small a dollar return they were getting for their effort.

Asked why he continues to grow vegetables, the onion braider will only say that he likes to work. But this is because he is hesitant to admit he is awed by his ability to turn bare ground green, by the way he can move his hands and bring forth abundance. Summer after summer, he has watched the garden fill up with foliage, until by fall he can never remember quite what it looked like when the snow melted. The corn, the beans, the pumpkins are all part of the change, but none delight him as much as the onions. They are so predictable. He has never had an onion failure. He has never heard of anyone else having one. Not with onion sets. Onions grow. He has come to count on it. It is this certainty that inspires him to give freely the extra attention that brings out their best. He cannot imagine a fall that did not include an afternoon in September when he sat on the ground braiding their hair.

Passalong Legacy

by Felder Rushing

When Granny died, I stole her chicken. Took it from her front yard while aunts and uncles were heavily into forensic financial discussions, divvying up the old woman's earthly possessions by familial rank and order.

I slipped out and quietly liberated the object that to me most nearly represented my grandmother's innermost style: an aged, paint-flaked concrete hen, her *Fiacre*, insouciant Guardian of Zinnias. Granny's sublime legacy.

What others had ridiculed as a frivolous ornament, I took as a heartfelt reminder of the over-looked oeuvre of a real, garden-variety gardener. Now it's in my own front yard, along with some of her bulbs and a paint bucketful of potted plants.

Granny was Sisyphus personified. No matter where she rolled her chicken around in her garden, she'd move it the next year. When the flowers looked good, the hen did, too; when the flowers were gone, the chicken made the emptiness more bearable.

Luckily, Granny's garden was small, just a suburban lotful of modest beds floating in a sea of St. Augustine grass. Most of the beds were surrounded with knee-high Walmart fencing reminiscent of the heavier antique "hairpin" style that used to be so common, and variegated monkey grass (Granny didn't care for Latin plant names, so when I think of her garden, neither do I). One bed had an antique urn bobbing in it—I stole that, too, along with the chicken. Couldn't help myself.

Granny loved flowers, though her garden style would have been mocked by the legions of preening designers who lecture to their cynical choir that "a collection of plants isn't a garden." Still, hers was genuine, coming from the heart, head, and hands of a real person making everyday choices. It wasn't designed to last forever.

Proust must have had Granny in mind when he wrote that "style is by no means an adornment . . . sit is a quality of vision, the revelation of the particular universe which each of us sees, and which is not seen by others." Her teeming Eden gave her as much pride as Du Pont got from Longwood—maybe more. To paraphrase Horton, Dr. Seuss's Whoville elephant, "A garden's a garden, no matter how small."

Granny's garden had home-rooted shrub roses and hydrangeas, and peonies, irises, periwinkle, orange daylilies, and "cut and come again" (which Mom and I decided was some sort of *Heliopsis*). And yarrow, passed from gardener to gardener for how many thousands of years now?

Every flower in Granny's collection was special, for several reasons. They had stories—trust me, interminable ones—in tow, giving them extra value. History is one of the most important of four basic "criteria" possessed by "passalong" plants.

Worth is an important value. Maybe a vegetable's seed is saved for generations because it's extra tasty. Or a flower is also useful as an herb or a cut flower. Perhaps it is kept around to signal seasonal change, like November *sasanquas* or summer gardenias. Or it's just pretty—a singularly good reason to keep a plant.

And fragrance is a memory jogger; jonquils never fail to take me back to my youth, spent in my great-grandmother's daffodil-filled garden. And while I'm watering my heartleaf philodendrons, rooted from "hospital plants" from when kids were born or a grandfather died, my past is conjured up. There are others, of course, and I get maudlin just thinking about them.

But fond memories, or any other measure of worth, can't keep a living, breathing plant going. For it to be cherished for long, a plant has to have an iron constitution, enough will to survive adverse soils, fickle climates, and sporadic care. It has to resist ordinary pests, at least have enough finesse to look good while under attack. If it's troublesome, or looks scraggly, out it goes.

For a plant to *really* succeed, it also has to be easy to propagate. Sharing the wealth spreads it out, keeps it going past the whims of fashion and through generations of benign neglect. Less chance of a crash wiping it out.

Some of my passalongs came my way honestly, some by way of my well-honed propagation sleight-of-hand. I'm faithfully sharing, though, trying to cheat my mortality, beat Sisyphus's eternal fate.

Granny's chicken, sadly out of place on my front deck, longs for the hairpin fence and roses. When I see it, my mind's eye sees a floriferous but long-gone garden; my wife, bless her heart, sees only a gaudy concrete ornament. (As if in her defense, movie director John Waters once said on late-night TV, "Good tacky looks up to its subject; bad tacky looks down.")

I'm trying to get past that artistic "eye of the beholder" stuff that makes one garden more acceptable than an other. Honestly (at the risk of being thought a garden-design Luddite), "horticulturally correct" gardens seem superficial—same old, same old, jazzed-up musty postcards. In southern gardens, "if it ain't ephemeral, it ain't real."

The flaking yellow chicken, now mine, looks forlorn in its new setting. We miss Granny, and we miss her zinnias.

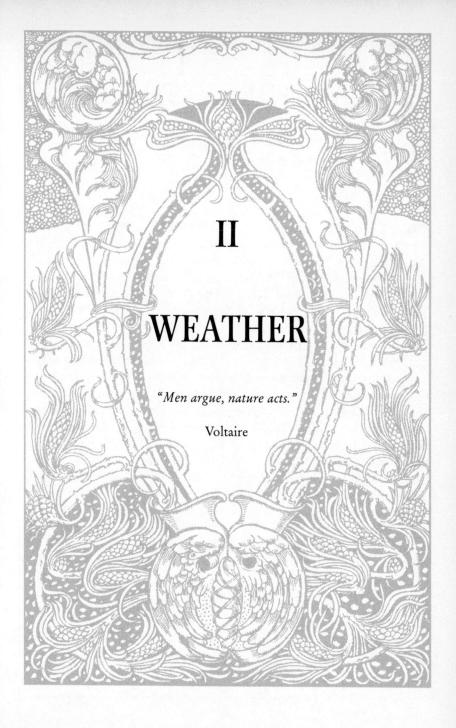

II

WEATHER

"Men argue, nature acts."

Voltaire

THE WEATHER IN THIS BOOK

from *The American Claimant*, 1892

by Mark Twain

No weather will be found in this book. This is an attempt to pull a book through without weather. It being the first attempt of the kind in fictitious literature, it may prove a failure, but it seemed worth the while of some daredevil person to try it, and the author was in just the mood.

Many a reader who wanted to read a tale through was not able to do it because of delays on account of the weather. Nothing breaks up an author's progress like having to stop every few pages to fuss up the weather. Thus it is plain that persistent intrusions of weather are bad for both reader and author.

Of course weather is necessary to a narrative of human experience. That is conceded. But it ought to be put where it will not be in the way; where it will not interrupt the flow of the narrative. And it ought to be the ablest weather that can be had, not ignorant, poor-quality, amateur weather. Weather is a literary specialty, and no untrained hand can turn out a good article of it. The present author can do only a few trifling ordinary kinds of weather, and he cannot do those very good. So it has seemed wisest to borrow such weather as is necessary for the book from qualified and recognized experts—giving credit, of course. The weather will be found over in the back part of the book, out of the way. See Appendix. The reader is requested to turn over and help himself from time to time as he goes along.

PREDICTING WEATHER

by Adele Q. Brown

Since man sowed his first seed and stalked his first prey, he has looked to to the animal, plant, and insect worlds, as well as to the sky, to predict the weather. While we now have Doppler 4000 radar at our disposal to relay the most minute shifts in wind and temperature, some argue that the accuracy of today's weather is no better than the folkloric wisdom of our astute ancestors.

Portents from the sky . . .

Stormy Weather:
- Red sky in the morning, sailors take warning.
- A morning rainbow indicates a westward rain will arrive.
- Three foggy mornings in a row signifies showers.
- Haziness around the sun means a storm is on its way.
- A halo around the moon is a sign of rain; the bigger the halo, the sooner the shower.
- If the stars twinkle excessively, expect precipitation.

Fair Weather:
- Red sky at night, sailors delight.
- An evening rainbow means that rain will pass to the east.
- Clear weather is certain when a patch of blue sky large enough to mend a Scotsman's jacket is seen in the northwest.
- If the full moon is clear on rising, expect clear weather.
- A sudden windshift in the midst of a storm indicates that fair weather is imminent.

From the plant kingdom . . .

- Morning glories, dandelions, daisies, white water lilies, wood sorrel, and wintergreen always close their blossoms before it rains.
- Flowers are noticeably more fragrant just before a rainfall.
- Moss that is moist and springy indicates rain; when it's dry and brittle, fair weather will remain.
- Sunflowers will raise their heads in anticipation of showers.
- Sugar maples turn their leaves upside down before rain.
- Copious berries and acorns foretell a cold winter.
- When you step on three daisies, spring has arrived.

and the animal kingdom . . .

- If a cat licks her fur against the grain, prepare for foul weather.
- A dog that eats grass in the morning foretells rain.
- Cows lying in a pasture portend a storm.
- When the squirrel is frisky in winter, the snow is almost over.
- If frogs croak more than usual, rain is near.
- Ants marching in columns indicate that a storm is coming. When they disperse, so will the storm.
- A cold winter is indicated by the crane's early arrival in autumn.
- When woodpeckers peck low on a tree, warmer weather is imminent.
- No killing frost will arrive after the martin comes to stay.
- If the cock goes crowing to bed, he'll certainly rise with a watery head.
- When the call of the phoebe is heard, the first traces of green and spring are not far behind.

Others predict weather through the calendar . . .

- A mild **January**, a chilly May.
- If **February** gives much snow, a fine summer it doth foreshow.
- The same amount of rain that falls in **March** will fall also in June.
- Thunder on **April** Fools' Day brings good crops of corn and hay.
- A cold **May** is kindly and fills the barn finely.
- A cold and wet **June** spoils the rest of the year.
- Never trust the sky in the month of **July**.
- If the 24th of **August** (St. Bartholomew's Day) be fair and clear, then hope for a prosperous autumn that year.
- If acorns are abundant on St. Michael's Day (**September** 29), there will be snow on the ground by Christmas.
- Warm **October**, cold February.
- If tree and grapevine leaves do not fall before **November** 11, then a cold winter is to be expected.
- A green **December** 25 means a heavy harvest.

Stormy Weather

by Adele Q. Brown

A State-by-State Storm-Disasters Guide

ALABAMA The worst winter storm in Alabama's history struck on March 12, 1993, and unleashed massive amounts of snow, high winds, lightning, and record-breaking cold costing over $100 million in damages. This storm was the beginning of the East Coast's "storm of the century," and in the period March 12–14, 1993, the greatest nontropical weather event in modern times occurred.

ALASKA Two records were set in Alaska on March 27, 1964, when the largest American earthquake of the century (9.2 on the Richter scale) rocked Prince William Sound, killing 115 people and generating $1.3 billion in damages, resulting mostly from landslides and tsunamis. One of these tidal waves was 220 feet high (roughly the height of a 20 story office building), thereby establishing a world record for the largest ever documented.

ARIZONA The state's worst heat wave occurred in Yuma, with temperatures above 100° every day in July 1959, topping out at 118°.

ARKANSAS The most devastating tornado eruption to hit Arkansas nearly obliterated Judsonia on March 21, 1952, when a 1 ½-mile-wide tornado left hundreds dead and only one structure unharmed: the church.

CALIFORNIA A 19-month drought preceding the 1970 Santa Ana winds fueled the most widespread brushfire in California history. In late September, fires raged through San Diego County, charring more than half a million acres and menacing Los Angeles suburbs and Sequoia National Park.

COLORADO Without warning on July 31, 1976, a thunderstorm began dumping rain on Big Thompson Canyon. With no place to go, the water rose in the narrow canyon, trapping inhabitants. The rushing torrent tossed homes, cars, and people against the canyon walls, killing 139.

CONNECTICUT On October 3, 1979, thunderstorms unexpectedly turned into deadly tornadoes in central Connecticut, cutting a 4-mile swath through Windsor and three other towns. More than 100 homes were damaged or destroyed, and 23 airplanes at the Bradley Air Museum were swept away.

DELAWARE In 1989 Delaware experienced one of its wettest summers on record. On July 5, 6.73 inches of rain fell on Wilmington in six hours, and by August 19, 26 roads had been closed after flooding wiped out 14 bridges.

FLORIDA Packing 145-mph winds and a 16.9-foot storm surge, Hurricane Andrew set a new American record for hurricane-related damages, outcosting 1989's Hurricane Hugo by 3.5 to 1 (see South Carolina). Andrew, which had stalked Florida as a Category 5 hurricane, came ashore at Biscayne Bay and Dade County on August 24, 1992, as a Category 4 tropical cyclone, inflicting $25 billion in damages and killing 23 people.

GEORGIA On the morning of April 6, 1936, 2 tornadoes, out of a 17-twister pack that had begun the night before, converged on Gainesville, leaving 203 dead, 70 of whom died in the Cooper Pants Factory, the largest death toll for a single building in a twister. Another 934 were injured and the town was left with $13 million in losses in Georgia's most tragic tornado outbreak.

HAWAII Iniki, the most potent hurricane to hit Hawaii in the 20th century, struck Kauai on September 11, 1992, just 18 days after Hurricane Andrew crushed southern Florida. Iniki was also Hawaii's costliest hurricane, delivering $4 billion worth of damage.

IDAHO In August 1910, 1,700 forest fires fueled by gale-force winds scorched a path 170 miles long and 15 miles wide through the national forests of Idaho's panhandle. This nightmare inferno, known as both the "Big Blowout" and the "Bitterroot Fires," burned 3 million acres of white pine and claimed the lives of 85 firefighters.

ILLINOIS America's deadliest tornado debacle occurred on March 18, 1925. Seven killer twisters, known as "The Tri-State Outbreak," descended, leaving 361 dead in Murphysboro and West Frankfurt. The leader of the pack traveled an unbelievable 219 miles from Missouri, across southern Illinois, and into Indiana.

INDIANA On December 9, 1917, a snowstorm originating in the Ohio Valley inundated Vevay with 26 inches of snow and 14-foot drifts. The cold continued, enabling residents to walk across the frozen Ohio River into Kentucky.

IOWA A staggeringly wet spring spawned The Great Flood of 1993. By July, parts of Des Moines were evacuated and 250,000 people were without water in the worst flood of the 20th century. Davenport was submerged and all bridges over the Mississippi between Iowa and St. Louis, Missouri, were closed. In all 70,000 people in nine states lost their homes, 20 million acres were uncultivatable, and $12 billion in losses were assessed.

KANSAS During the Great Drought of 1988–89, Kansas received only 5 inches of precipitation in 7 months and had below-average precipitation for 16 months in a row, from February 1988 to May 1989. The wheat yield in Kansas, the number-one wheat-producing state in the nation, fell to 35 percent, its lowest in 22 years. The Great Drought affected at least a dozen states and topped Hurricane Andrew (see Florida) as the most expensive natural disaster in U.S. history, with losses estimated in excess of $40 billion.

KENTUCKY As thunderstorms raced through the state on November 15, 1989, 3-inch hail stones fell in Grayson County and winds reached 110 mph near Fort Knox.

LOUISIANA On June 27, 1957, Hurricane Audrey landed at Cameron, demolishing all but one brick and one cement building. Audrey, the deadliest June hurricane ever, produced a 12 foot storm surge that traveled 25 miles upriver, drowning 390 people along its path. Oil rigs in the Gulf were battered by 180-mph winds, and a 70-ton boat was lifted out of the water onto an offshore platform.

MAINE On November 21, 1989, a blizzard, which dumped 18 inches of snow on Vanceboro and produced hurricane-force winds on the coast and 58-mph gusts inland at Augusta, was responsible for 35 storm-related injuries.

MARYLAND By August 11, the 1988 summer heat wave that roasted Baltimore had produced a record-breaking 14 consecutive 90° days. By August 18, 13 days of 100° temperatures for the year had been documented.

MASSACHUSETTS A paralyzing ice storm gripped New England on November 28, 1921, when over 3 inches of ice fell, followed by 2 feet of snow. Worcester's population was immobilized when gale force winds combined with freezing rain made travel treacherous and caused power and telephone outages. Damages were estimated at $20 million.

MICHIGAN On November 10, 1975, one day and 62 years after a deadly "freshwater fury" on Lake Erie killed 270 sailors, another cyclone over water struck Michigan. This time the "freshwater fury" occurred over Lake Superior, and 29 men died as the *Edmund Fitzgerald* sunk off Crisp Point.

MINNESOTA A nor'easter lashed Lake Superior with 73-mph winds, causing 20- to 40-foot waves and flooding Grand Marais and the northern shore of Lake Superior on November 28, 1960.

MISSISSIPPI Hurricane Camille was the most powerful storm to hit the Gulf Coast and only the second Category 5 hurricane to strike the United States when it made landfall at Pass Christian on August 17, 1969. Its 24 foot storm surge was the highest ever recorded in the U.S. history, its winds were in excess of 200 mph, and its sheer intensity pushed tides 3 feet above normal for over 125 miles to the east of the hurricane's impact. By the time it was over, Camille had killed 256, demolished 5,500 homes, damaged 12,500 others, and destroyed 700 businesses.

MISSOURI Heavy rains from April storms in southern Missouri contributed to the Great Mississippi Flood of 1927. Already at flood stage, the Mississippi and Ohio Rivers overflowed, breaking 120 levees in seven states. Over 80 miles wide in some places, the Mississippi's floodwaters forced more than half a million people from their homes, flooded 260,000 square miles, and took 246 lives.

MONTANA Temperatures plummeted a startling 100° in just 24 hours on January 24, 1916, setting a U.S. record in Browning when the mercury dropped from 46° above zero to 54° below zero.

NEBRASKA On Easter Sunday, March 23, 1913, a killer tornado, witnessed by train passengers paralleling the storm, made a direct hit on Ralston before taking aim at downtown Omaha, killing 154 and razing all structures in a seven-block radius. A freak blizzard two days later hampered rescue work, while damaging fires ravaged the city and its suburbs.

NEVADA After 137 days of drought, Las Vegas received measurable precipitation on January 2, 1990, for the first time since August 1989.

NEW HAMPSHIRE After sustaining an average speed of 186 mph for five minutes, the wind blew at the highest speed ever recorded in the world on April 20, 1934, gusting to 231 mph atop Mount Washington.

NEW JERSEY On September 14, the Hurricane of 1944 roared up the eastern seaboard at 30 mph, demolished Atlantic City's boardwalk, and sank numerous boats, killing 344 at sea and another 46 on land.

NEW MEXICO A U.S. record for the coldest temperature in the month of April was reported at Eagles Nest, where on April 5, 1989, the mercury bottomed out at 45° below zero.

NEW YORK After a three-day blizzard that began on January 28, 1977, buried Buffalo under 45 inches of snow, severe winds caused 25-foot snow drifts and sent windchill temperatures plunging to 50° below zero.

NORTH CAROLINA When Hurricane Fran struck on September 5, 1996, it was the second billion-dollar hurricane to hit North Carolina in seven years and the 16th hurricane to hit the Cape Fear area in the twentieth century. Over one million people were left without power, $5 billion in damages was reported, and 38 deaths were attributed to the storm.

NORTH DAKOTA Forty-five years to the day after setting a record for the longest sequence of consecutive daily subzero temperatures, Bismarck tied the old record of 45 days on February 10, 1982.

OHIO The Super Outbreak of Tornadoes that ravaged 11 states in 12 hours from the afternoon of April 3 through the early-morning hours of April 4, 1974, spawned more F5 tornadoes (winds over 261 mph) in one day than normally occur in a decade. One of the 148 twisters in the outbreak wiped out half of Xenia, east of Dayton, killing 34. School buses were hurled through high school walls and trains were lifted off their tracks as if they were toys.

OKLAHOMA Severe heat bursts—high winds accompanied by rapid temperature rises—were reported in ten Southwest counties from the evening of May 22, 1996, through the early morning of May 23. Temperatures skyrocketed from 87° to 101° in 25 minutes in Chickasha, while wind gusts of 105 mph downed power lines and sent barn roofs sailing.

OREGON Flooding in the Willamette Basin region on February 9, 1996 was the worst since the Christmas Flood of December 24, 1964. Above-normal temperatures caused snowmelts that combined with rains from a subtropical storm, forced rivers 7 to 10 feet above flood stage. Seven deaths and $700 million in property and highway damages resulted.

PENNSYLVANIA By February 18, 1996, Philadelphia had broken two storm records for snowfall: the most ever (30.7 inches) in one storm as the result of the January 6–8 blizzard; and the greatest seasonal record for snow (55.5 inches). The subsequent snowmelt caused some of the worst flooding since 1972's Hurricane Agnes, with over $1 billion in losses.

RHODE ISLAND The Hurricane of 1938 was the most violent tropical cyclone to tear into the Northeast in the 20th century. Its spectacular speed of 70 mph and last-minute shift in direction caught northerners by surprise. The storm surge was so powerful that it carried water upriver to the second floors in central Providence. Coastal homes were ripped off their foundations, trees were uprooted, and severe floods washed out entire portions of New England, killing over 600 people in the fourth-deadliest hurricane to hit the United States.

SOUTH CAROLINA On September 21–22, 1989, Hurricane Hugo bombarded Charleston with 135-mph winds. The Category 4 hurricane was the most powerful to strike the United States in 30 years, a berth it would occupy for only 3 years before being supplanted by Hurricane Andrew in 1992 (see Florida).

SOUTH DAKOTA Spearfish was the site of the most sensational temperature rise in the world on January 22, 1943, when the temperature rose 49° in only two minutes from 4° below zero to 45° above. One hour later the temperature dropped from 54° above zero to 4° below in 27 minutes.

TENNESSEE Two crippling early February ice storms engulfed Tennessee first in 1951 and then again in 1994. In 1951, 25 people died in the storm, which left 4 inches of ice throughout the South. In 1994 three-quarters of a million Tennessee residents were left without electricity, some for a month, and damages were five times the 1951 figure of $100 million. The 1994 storm's total regional cost was estimated at $3.5 billion. Shelbyville recorded an unbelievable 7.7 inches of ice.

TEXAS The greatest loss of life from any natural disaster in the United States occurred in Galveston on September 8, 1900. On that day a fierce Category 4 hurricane hit the island, producing a 20-foot storm surge and a 15-foot tide, submerging the island under Gulf and Bay waters, ripping apart brick and wood buildings, and killing over 7,200 people, approximately 19 percent of Galveston's population.

UTAH A single storm on January 25, 1965, set a state record for snowfall when Alta was buried under 105 inches of white powder.

VERMONT The dust storm that inaugurated the Dust Bowl era of the 1930s was carried eastward and fell on Vermont as brown snow on November 13, 1933.

VIRGINIA On March 3, 1962, the combination of "Spring Tides" and a sustained bombardment of onshore winds of up to 70 mph and 40-foot waves brought about an incredible tidal flooding that shifted Virginia's coastline.

WASHINGTON After 120 years of inactivity, Mount St. Helens erupted in the early-morning hours of May 18, 1980, spewing volcanic debris 14 miles into the air-darkened skies and fell to earth as thick ash up to 100 miles east of the explosion. Despite seismic activity earlier in the month, the volcanic eruption caught Washington off guard, and the force and severity of the resultant devastation were staggering; debris cascaded down the mountain at 100 mph, annihilating forests, obliterating homes, and killing at least 65.

WEST VIRGINIA A deadly tornado nearly wiped out the hilltop town of Shinnston on June 23, 1944, upsetting the previously held belief that mountainous regions were impervious to tornadoes. Over 150 people perished in this and three parallel twisters that struck the same day.

WISCONSIN During the national heat wave of 1988, Milwaukee had braved 34 days of 90° and above temperatures by mid-August.

WYOMING So much hail fell to the ground on August 11, 1987, that snowplows were brought out of summer storage to remove the 2-foot high drifts of golf-ball-size hail that had accumulated on Highway 24 near Hulett.

Storm Glossary

FUJITA SCALE: Named after T. Theodore Fujita, the physicist who devised this methodology, the scale is a measurement of a tornado's wind velocity, and hence the storm's severity, using the following shorthand: F0 is a Gale Tornado, winds 42–72 mph.

> F1 is a Moderate Tornado, winds 73–112 mph.
> F2 is a Significant Tornado, winds 113–157 mph.
> F3 is a Severe Tornado, winds 158–206 mph.
> F4 is a Devastating Tornado, winds 207–260 mph.
> F5 is an Incredible Tornado, winds 261–318 mph.

HAIL: Stones of ice formed in the updrafts of thunderstorms, hail pieces are usually larger than $\frac{1}{4}$ inch in diameter and in some extreme instances can grow to the size of a softball.

HURRICANE: A hurricane is a nonfrontal cyclone whose winds, rotating in a counterclockwise direction around a center, exceed 74 mph. Because hurricanes begin in tropical waters, they are also referred to as tropical cyclones (see below). The intensity of a hurricane is measured by the Saffir-Simpson scale (see below). In the North Pacific, west of the international date line, a hurricane is knows as a typhoon.

NOR'EASTER: This storm is similar to a hurricane because it is borne out of a low-pressure system and its winds rotate in a counterclockwise direction around a center. Nor'easters differ from hurricanes in that they are not tropical in origin but take form in temperate climates and are transported to the northeast by the jetstream. While hurricanes strike in summer or early fall, nor'easters wreak their havoc in winter and spring. Unlike a hurricane, which has pinpoint strength upon impact, a nor'easter can ravage a widespread area for days, mostly along the coast.

SAFFIR-SIMPSON SCALE: This is a measurement of a hurricane's potential severity that was developed by Herbert Saffir and Robert Simpson in order to predict damages by categorizing the storm in terms of its intensity as a combination of wind speed, barometric pressure, and storm surge as in the following table.

	Wind Speed	Barometric Pressure	Storm Surge
Category 1	74–95 mph	28.94"	4–5'
Category 2	96–110 mph	28.50-28.91"	6–8'
Category 3	111–130 mph	27.91-28.47"	9–12'
Category 4	131–155 mph	27.17-27.88"	13–18'
Category 5	over 155 mph	below 27.17"	over 18'

STORM SURGE: Mistakenly referred to as a "tidal wave" in years past, a storm surge is the growing mound of water that accrues as a hurricane moves over water and approaches land. As the hurricane strikes, it unleashes this increased level of water, causing massive shore damage, erosion, and flooding. It is the flooding from the storm surge that is a hurricane's number-one killer.

TIDAL WAVE: While this term is interchangeable with "tsunami" (see below) it had been previously used inaccurately to describe what is now referred to as a storm surge (see above).

TORNADO: This is a storm funnel formed by a downward rotating vortex originating in thunderclouds becomes a forceful and destructive twister when it touches the ground. The counterclockwise-circulating winds can blow from 50 to 300 mph, last from seconds to hours, be a few yards or nearly half a mile wide, and travel a distance of a few feet or hundreds of miles. Their destructiveness is measured by the Fujita scale (see above).

TROPICAL CYCLONE: A tropical cyclone is any low-pressure storm without fronts in the Atlantic Basin, the Pacific Ocean east of the international date line, the Indian Ocean, or the Coral Sea whose winds rotate in a counterclockwise direction around a central core warmer than the surrounding air. When winds are measured between 39 and 74 mph, the tropical cyclone reaches tropical storm status. Above 74 mph, the tropical cyclone becomes a hurricane (see above).

TSUNAMI: This Japanese word describes more accurately than "tidal wave" the wall of seawater that comes ashore in the aftermath of suboceanic seismic activity. Tsunamis are devastatingly powerful and destructive and can be 100 feet or more in height.

TYPHOON: See Hurricane.

Odd Weather Disasters and Trivia

- A man carrying 35 sticks of dynamite was struck by lightning on September 24, 1972, in Waldport, Oregon, and was blown to smithereens.

- The only official death by hail was recorded in Lubbock, Texas, on May 13, 1930, when the unfortunate victim was trapped in an open field without protection.

- On July 6, 1928, a hailstone weighing 1½ pounds and measuring 17 inches in circumference and 5 ½ inches in diameter was discovered after a storm in Potter, Nebraska.

- When lightning hit a transformer in Utah on July 6, 1985, most of the state was plunged into darkness and a 200-foot fireball lit up the Salt Lake County sky.

- Two million chickens died in Alabama as a result of a snowstorm on January 7, 1988 that produced 27 inches of snow.

- On August 28, 1959, Lt. Col. William Rankin bailed out of his faltering airplane at 46,000 feet into a thunderstorm. His descent to earth took 45 excruciating minutes as Rankin was violently tossed about by the storm clouds.

- On November 7, 1951, a fireball descended to earth accompanied by a horrific roar heard in Texas, Oklahoma, and Kansas, which was apparently caused by a disintegrating meteor.

- A tornado on January 18, 1973, in Corey, Louisiana picked up a baby and carried him over 300 yards but left the boy virtually unharmed.

- A million turkeys being readied for Thanksgiving were smothered on November 8, 1943, when 2 feet of snow unexpectedly fell in South Dakota.

- Dead ducks dropped from the sky in Great Bend, Kansas, after a deadly autumn tornado struck the farm community on November 10, 1915.

- A dog landed unharmed in a treetop after a tornado had carried it half a mile from its kennel in Munising, Michigan, on July 9, 1987.

- Lightning struck a fish farm on April 20, 1990, in Scott, Arkansas, and all 10,000 pounds of live fish perished from the heat of the subsequent fire.

- Park ranger Roy C. Sullivan was struck by lightning for the seventh time on June 26, 1977.

- In August 1993 a man riding on horseback on the Wasatch Plateau in Emory County, Utah, was struck on the crown of the head by lightning. One bolt traveled around his neck, followed a zig zag line down his abdomen, and exited his body 2 inches above the groin. A second bolt traversed his left leg, exiting above his knee. He had severe exit-wound gashes and his stomach lining was burned. The horse he was riding was killed instantly.

- The first two weeks of March 1993 were so wet in four counties of Idaho that there was an above-average mortality rate for newborn calves caused by "weather stress."

- During the March 12–13 "storm of the century," in 1993, Cutler, Maine was hit with such fierce winds that waves off the coast carried "ice cakes" to shore. This resulted in 2 ½ miles of clam beds being plowed up, exposing billions of clams in Little Machias Bay.

- On May 23, 1992, in Success, Arkansas, a woman stopped her car to adjust her windshield wipers. Lightning that had struck a nearby utility pole traveled through the ground, encircling her. She was temporarily paralyzed in her right arm and leg but recovered completely in a few days.

- Apparently undeterred by the thunderstorm outside, a boy playing Nintendo® inside his house was unaware that lightning had struck a 30-foot cottonwood tree in his backyard, arced to the water meter on the side of the house, and then traveled through the piping in his home to the living room, where a fire broke out while he was occupied with his game.

Zeroing In on Your Microclimate

by Charlotte M. Frieze

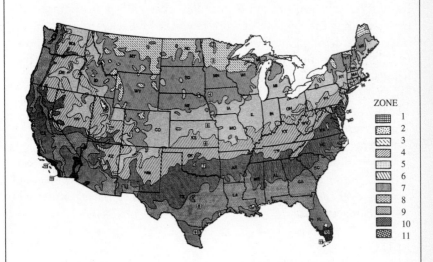

ZONE
1
2
3
4
5
6
7
8
9
10
11

W hile real estate agents are famous for chanting "location, location, location," the gardener's mantra should be "climate, climate, climate." A garden in sync with its climate will look like Main Street has been transformed into a verdant paradise.

To begin, locate your climate zone on the USDA Plant Hardiness Zone map. This is the starting point to selecting plants that will survive in your zone. But because survival alone will not lead to a bountiful garden, zero in on your microclimates and give your plants what they need to thrive. A microclimate is a small area where growing conditions differ from the overall climate. They occur when climatic, natural, and man-made elements converge; a multitude can exist within the boundaries of your property.

Microclimates can be extremely useful when you are selecting and siting plants for your unique growing conditions. In cooler zones, exploit warm pockets to extend the growing season, to grow more tender or sun-loving plants, and to protect special plants against an unexpectedly brutal winter. Reserve cold pockets for the hardiest plants. In warm zones, set aside cool pockets for heat-sensitive plants, hot spots for an early-spring garden. In all zones, save wet spots for thirsty plants and dry areas for drought-tolerant plants.

Walk around your property during the different seasons, looking for sun traps, warm or cold winds, and areas with poor drainage. By understanding the elements at work in your own backyard, you can tailor your gardening practices to where you live. Work with the following elements to find the perfect spot for that favorite rose or other beloved plant.

TEMPERATURE

Temperature determines your hardiness zone and growing season by influencing the critical plant processes of photosynthesis, transpiration, and respiration. Enclosing a garden with hedges or walls can raise the temperature within the garden by blocking the wind; conversely, the wind blowing over the surfaces of pools, ponds, and other water features will lower temperatures.

ALTITUDE

Altitude can be a major factor in determining your zone. For every 250 feet above sea level, the temperature drops about 1°F. With only a 10° difference between zones, a high site may well be in the next colder zone.

FROST

Frost is frozen moisture. It forms on plants when air temperatures drop below 32°F and in the soil when ground temperatures drop below freezing. Beware of frost pockets, particularly if your home is on a hillside. Cold air naturally flows downhill like water, and if blocked by a hill, wall, or building, it will spread out and up, forming air or frost pockets that, like water, can freeze and damage roots. To minimize frost damage, make sure cold air keeps moving through the garden, and avoid planting tender plants in any known frost pockets.

SNOW

Gardeners in cold climates welcome a winter blanket of snow, as it provides excellent insulation from often dramatic temperature fluctuations. It can also prevent excessive frost heaving, which can push shallow-rooted plants out of the ground. Properly winterize your garden to counter the effects of tough, snowless winters.

RAINFALL

Farmers worry about rainfall and you should, too. If you live near the ocean or the Great Lakes, you generally enjoy increased rainfall, but for those living farther inland, rainfall may be irregular. In all climates, pick plants that are compatible with your annual rainfall, and if you are away from the garden for long periods, make provisions with a neighbor to water should an unexpected hot spell arise.

DRAINAGE

Adequate drainage is just as important as a steady supply of water. Too much water, or waterlogging, decreases the amount of air in the soil. Air provides oxygen and insulation for the roots. A high water table will draw roots up to the surface, where they are susceptible to cold; deep roots are well insulated from frost.

HUMIDITY

Humidity is water vapor in the air and moisture in the soil and is beneficial to plants such as ferns, but it can cause severe fungal growth. If your garden is in a humid area, select plants that are adapted to high humidity or look for the mold-resistant strains of many popular perennials that are now available. And don't crowd your plants; good air circulation will help reduce unwanted levels of humidity.

SUNLIGHT

The intensity of the sun varies at different times of the day. The midday sun is the hottest, followed by the afternoon and then the morning sun. Remember that light requirements may be affected by climatic conditions. A perennial that needs full sun in Zone 5 may perform better in partial shade in Zone 7.

Take advantage of protected sunny spots; they may be able to support plants of a higher zone. To extend the growing season or to establish a spring garden, plant on the south side of the house. But beware of the drying western sun; your soil may require additional water.

WIND

We appreciate a cooling breeze on a hot summer day, and plants do, too. It disperses their pollen and seeds, prevents pockets of stagnant air in the garden, and dries off the morning dew inhibiting fungal growth. However, wind can dehydrate leaves just as it dries laundry on a line. A plant on a windy hilltop, on the open plains, or along the coast will have to work harder to provide a steady supply of water to the leaves, which may result in diminished growth.

Wind can also lower temperature. If your home is on a windy hillside, your garden may be a Zone 5, while your friend's protected garden down the road may be a Zone 6.

Climate is at the heart of the garden. Armed with an understanding of your microclimates, you can achieve peak performance in your garden by selecting the right plant for the right place and even experiment successfully with plants beyond your zone. And you can do it with less effort than you think.

WEATHER

by Roger B. Swain

In our judgment of the weather, we have become exceptionally narrow-minded. The forecaster on the radio this morning issued a "winter storm warning," and if the predicted flakes materialize, a couple of inches of accumulation will create a "state of emergency." Last summer this same forecaster persisted in describing possible showers, in the middle of a drought, as a "threat of rain." The only precipitation that is greeted with any enthusiasm these days is snow on Christmas Eve. Otherwise, "good" weather means sunny, mild, and dry.

If the issue were to appear on a ballot, the majority of the nation's populace would, I suspect, vote to severely restrict rain, mist, fog, hail, sleet, snow, and ice. High winds would certainly be outlawed. I can imagine minimum temperatures being set state by state, figures roughly equal to the highway speed limits in effect before the price of oil went up. And local ordinances allowing the presence of a few clouds of the fair-weather sort, and now and then a gentle breeze or heavy dew.

At present, however, the weather remains outside our regulatory discretion. When the skies cloud over and the mercury falls, we can either move indoors or move away. Each year more people join the geese and head south, some for the winter, some for good. The ones who stay behind will spend the winter lamenting the cost of home heating. By spring we will be suffering to varying extents from cabin fever, the result of being cooped up too long.

Outside the kitchen window, chickadees are pulling flower seeds from the feeder. Part of the entertainment for us is the marvel of such small bundles of feathers surviving the weather. But is the weather all that bad? I think we have set our thermostats too high. In Tierra del Fuego, midsummer temperatures average 45°F by day, and yet Charles Darwin noted there in his journal of December 25,

1832, that he had seen a woman nursing a newborn baby, both mother and child apparently oblivious to the sleet that fell and thawed on their naked bodies. A month later he wrote that while others of his party huddled around the fire for warmth, undressed Fuegians positioned at some distance were "streaming with perspiration at undergoing such a roasting."

This tolerance of cold comes from long acclimation. It is not something we can acquire overnight. But our intolerance is also the fruit of years of conditioning. Each of us has been taught to believe that we could never survive such exposure, that wet feet and cold hands are sure to bring on illness—a "cold in the nose" or a "cold in the head." As children we knew better. We spent all day out sledding or ran about in the rain, ignoring our mother's warnings that we would catch double pneumonia. And we survived.

Some weather is undeniably bad for you. We do well to avoid hurricanes, tornadoes, and electrical storms. But we should not balk at rain and snow. If the day turns out to be cold or wet, we don't have to cancel our plans to spend it outdoors. With an extra wool sweater or two, and some boot grease in winter, a broad-brimmed hat and a slicker in summer, even those accustomed to the shelter of climate-controlled buildings can return to their youth and safely venture outside.

Raindrops falling on the open water of a lily pond, salamanders crossing a path on a rainy night. The cold squeak of snow underfoot, sea smoke in the bay on a frigid morning. Once in a great while, an entire grove of spruce transformed by ice into a giant crystal chandelier. These are the transitory beauties of bad weather, the bounty of those who are broad-minded.

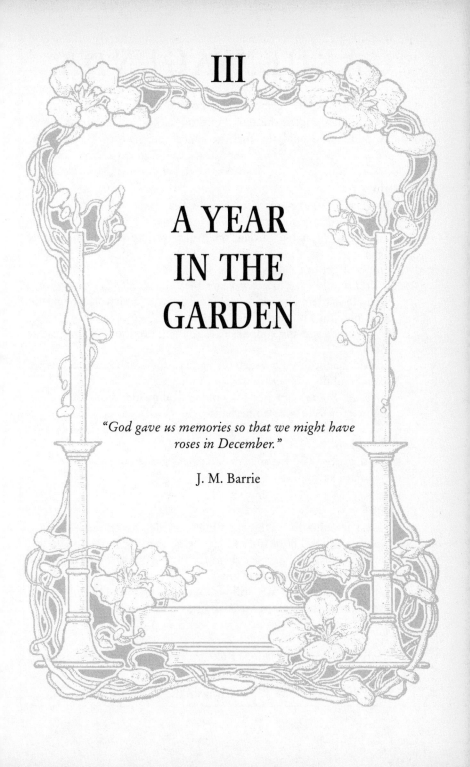

III

A YEAR
IN THE
GARDEN

"God gave us memories so that we might have roses in December."

J. M. Barrie

GARDEN AGENDA

by Elizabeth L. Haskins

January

- Surf the Internet for gardening websites.
- Peruse seed catalogs.
- Plan your vegetable garden; try a new variety of squash or pole beans.
- Don't forget to rotate your crops!
- If you would love to grow vegetables and don't have room for a separate garden, choose ornamental varieties and work them into your perennial border.
- Order seeds and any supplies that you will need to start your seeds indoors.
- To add height to your vegetable garden this year, construct a tepee from bamboo, copper tubing, or branches.
- To grow home remedies for common ailments, look for a class, seminar, or lecture by an herbalist.
- Use sand instead of salt on icy walkways if they are near your lawn or garden.
- For the new year, consider making your garden organic.
- Dream of spring!

February

- Visit a greenhouse in a nearby botanic garden for an early spring.
- Go to your local bookstore to see the new spring gardening books.
- Survey your tools, prepare them for their new season, and replace any that no longer do their job.
- While your plants are still dormant, prune summer-blooming shrubs, fruit trees, grapevines, and berry bushes.

March

- It's time for spring cleanup! Rake up any twigs and leaves and add them to your compost pile.
- Begin removing your winter protection.

- Cut back any perennials that were left standing for the winter.
- Collect tree branches or large twigs to be used as bean or perennial supports.
- Prune deciduous hedges.
- If you have a cover crop in your vegetable garden, turn it under and prepare the soil for planting.
- Weather permitting, sow your peas.

April

- As the foliage from your bulbs begins to peek out, apply a bulb fertilizer.
- Rake and prepare your annual bed for planting.
- After the last frost, prune your roses and feed them with compost.
- For many of us, it's finally time to think about—or even shop for—annuals. Plan your color scheme and try to find at least one new variety that self-sows.

May

- Divide your fall- and winter-blooming perennials.
- To encourage your peonies to produce one big flower per stem, disbud all but the terminal bud.
- Call your local garden club for a schedule of the garden tours offered this spring.
- Plan a party for June—your garden will be in peak season.
- Feed your roses and scratch a tablespoon or so of Epsom salts around each bush.
- If you have roses and like bananas, bury the peels near your rosebushes—the potassium will give your roses a boost.
- If wasps are a problem, buy wasp traps and place them away from your picnic table.

June

- Visit a favorite botanic garden and don't miss the rose garden there.
- Prune your spring-blooming shrubs after they have flowered.
- Go strawberry picking at a nearby farm.
- If you are planning on preserving berries this year, have your canning jars and favorite recipes on hand.
- Turn your favorite fruit into sorbet.

July

- Deadhead your roses.
- If your perennials look tired, cut them back!
- Set your grill up in the garden; invite friends over for vegetables grilled with fresh herbs.
- Pick beans often to improve production.
- As an accompaniment for grilled fish, chicken, meat, or vegetables, chop fresh herbs, mix with softened butter, and pack in crocks. This will keep in the refrigerator for at least two weeks.

August

- Lounge at least once in your hammock.
- Browse through gardening catalogs or visit your local nursery for fall plantings of bulbs and peonies.
- If you've got an abundance of cucumbers, try making pickles this year.
- If you're planning on adding a new perennial bed next year, it's a good idea to dig and amend the bed the season before.
- Remove spent annuals and add them to your compost pile.

September

- If you live in a cold-winter area, stop feeding your roses.
- Make pesto, trying a new recipe this year.
- If you haven't had your soil tested, or if your garden didn't perform the way you had hoped, have your soil tested. This will give you a chance to amend the soil and let it settle before next season.
- Divide your spring- and summer-blooming perennials.

October

- Harvest your herbs and use them to make vinegar, mustards, or potpourri for the holiday season.
- It's time for apple picking and apple cider!
- Amend the soil in your vegetable garden with compost and lime if necessary. Plant a cover crop, such as winter rye.
- Fertilize your existing bulbs and plant new ones.
- If you garden in a northern climate, lift and store your tender bulbs.

- To bring your garden indoors, plan to force bulbs in ornamental pots or bowls. Good bulbs for forcing include tulips, amaryllis, muscari, hyacinths, scilla, and narcissus.
- If you're planning on a live Christmas tree this year, prepare a planting hole.
- Visit a local pumpkin patch. When you carve your pumpkin, remove the seeds, clean them, and bake on an oiled cookie sheet.
- Make a vat of squash or pumpkin soup from a new recipe. Enjoy, and freeze the remainder to get you through the winter.

November

- Make a wreath, topiary, or dried flower arrangement for the holidays.
- Visit your local bookstore to explore the new Christmas gardening books on display. (Your newspaper most likely will be reviewing their favorites.)
- Cut back the perennials that no longer add interest to the garden. Cover with a layer of compost.
- Check with your local garden club or botanic garden for a class or lecture.
- If you have climbing roses, tie up any vulnerable canes so they won't be damaged in the wind.
- Mound soil and compost around plants such as roses that are vulnerable to the cold.
- Rake up any remaining leaves from your beds and add them to your compost pile.
- If winter temperatures drop below freezing in your region, drain your hoses and store them. Drain faucets and shut the water off.
- If gardening was more work than fun this year, consider downsizing your garden, or set a more realistic goal for next year.

December

- Oil and clean your tools; sharpen the blades of your pruners.
- Store your tools in a bucket of sand mixed with vegetable oil.
- Using dried herbs—your own or from a market—prepare vinegar or mustard to give as holiday gifts.

THE ASTROLOGICAL GARDENER

by Nina Straus

ARIES (March 21–April 19)
As the first sign in the zodiac, Aries is associated with the element of fire, the masculine force of Mars, and the principle of first growth. Aries gardeners prefer hardy impatiens to hybrid tea roses; spring bulbs such as narcissus, tulips, or daffodils to shy violets. Their penchant for quick-growing vegetables (carrots, scallions) that go from garden to table into the mouth suggest Aries' impulsiveness. Throw on the seeds, dig plants into the earth! Let them come forth!

TAURUS (April 20–May 20)
Those born under the sign of Taurus stand firm by gardens that express patience and comfort. As a fixed earth sign ruled by Venus, Taurus is the "green thumb" position. Composting may be a habit. There is a preference for plants that are reliable. Vegetable gardens and orchards are stuffed with delicious fruits and vegetables brought to a well-equipped kitchen at the ripest moment. Flower gardens display pink and blue phlox, violets, sensual peonies, and bush roses—traditional varieties that suggest how everything can be accomplished in the fullness of time.

GEMINI (May 21–June 20)
As the sign of the twins, Gemini is associated with air and ruled by the mutable spirit of Mercury. Geminis play both sides of their flower beds and approach their gardens as problems to be solved. The results are interesting, with gardens that may change from year to year: one summer all exotic herbs, the next a shift to 10 varieties of lupine. Geminis may create gardens to contain their conflicting impulses: one section exhibiting yellow calla lilies flanked by a rise of blue heather, another section all lettuce and peas.

CANCER (June 21–July 22)
With their watery, sensitive, and maternal spirits ruled by the moon, Cancer gardeners coddle and protect their plants. They never forget bird netting mesh to protect butterfly trees throughout the winter. Climbing roses and clematis are guaranteed the support of walls. Flower beds are usually near the house, and pastel geraniums in window boxes signal a love for domestic security. Cancer gardeners enjoy fertilizing their soil. They may overwater their cauliflower in a zeal to nourish. Incorporating a round garden containing white digitalis and white lilies in the landscape, Cancers tread with care in their moonlit spaces.

LEO (July 23–August 22)
Born under a fixed fire sign ruled by the sun, Leos stage their gardens for dramatic effect. They need theaters of gold marigolds and red hibiscus, or driveways flanked by orange rhododendrons leading up to a flush of perennials with names like 'King' and 'Imperial' (roses) and 'Hyperion' (lilies). If possible, Leo gardens will be set out on a hill for the world to admire. The ostentatious spirit shows itself even in a modest vegetable patch of corn and peppers where a crescent of sunflowers or a feather-leaved red maple takes center stage.

VIRGO (August 23–September 22)
Virgos are mutable earth signs ruled by Mercury. Their interest in health and order creates gardens as refuges of sanity where medicinal herbs can be clipped for use. Virgos critique and organize their gardens. Neat borders and constant pruning are a necessity. Tool storage racks (no clutter) are found in their vicinities. Colors and sizes of flowers tend to be coordinated and elegant. Virgo tomatoes are cleanly staked and standing in strict rows. Plants will be grown according to schedule, guaranteeing that something will be blooming and ripening throughout the season. As for weeds and mold, Japanese beetles and deadheads: they are banished as soon as they appear.

LIBRA (September 23–October 22)
Libras, air signs ruled by Venus and Saturn, balance their gardens. Harmony of color and structure is achieved without showing the strain. Flower gardens contain perennials such as bush roses and astilbes. Vegetable gardens offer sweet-smelling herbs but nothing that demands elaborate staking and fumigating. Libras do not like difficult plants that

require struggle. A birdbath and a well-placed chair, bench, or hammock for resting coordinate Libran gardening pleasures for a total effect.

SCORPIO (October 23–November 21)
Scorpios, fixed water signs ruled by Mars and Pluto, indulge and control their gardens. They give no quarter to pests. Flower gardens may look perfectly traditional until one discovers the (pitch black) 'Night Owl' iris lurking behind the morning glories or the steely blue balls of echinops planted beside the spider lilies. Scorpios like drama and simplicity: stones and sand with a burst of blood red Oriental poppies surrounded by empty space. Contrast and mystery, even in the vegetable garden (the purple broccoli next to the white eggplant), is the way their gardens go.

SAGITTARIUS (November 22–December 21)
As mutable fire signs ruled by Jupiter, Sagittarian gardeners urge their plants onward and upward. These gardeners go for sky-thrusting spiky flowers such as hollyhocks, phlox, heathers, and veronica. Gardens may be planted far from the house so the Sagittarian can journey to get there. A haphazard quality, a mix of colors, and a spilling over of borders make the garden lively and generous, if not always neat. Vegetable gardens contain the successes as well as the failures, often the result of giving pests an overdose of Sagittarian love of liberty. These gardens may also contain more than a few experiments.

CAPRICORN (December 22–January 19)
As earth signs ruled by Saturn, Capricorns push their plants on to greater achievements. The key word for their gardens is structure.
Capricorns number their gardens among their status symbols and buy expensive plant varieties. Rare hybrid tea roses, fruit trees, and a powerful show of chrysanthemums fill out a well-organized landscape. Because Capricorns are also practical, their vegetable gardens are productive, well weeded, and protected with a high and durable fence.

AQUARIUS (January 20–February 18)
Ruled by Saturn and Uranus, Aquarians use their gardens as experiment stations. They grow orchids under fluorescent light bulbs, using soil thermometers. Or they employ solar-powered compost tumblers outside to nourish amaryllis with the proper technology. Aquarians prefer iridescent-colored flowers and original kinds of vegetables. Gardens are the

place to stimulate and satisfy curiosity, to exercise pruning skills and implements, and to gather with friends.

PISCES (February 19–March 20)
As mutable water signs ruled by Neptune, Pisces hide in their gardens to contemplate love and life. Ponds or fountains are as important as flowers. Paths lead to secret nooks. Emotional expressiveness prevails: bleeding hearts, heavenly blue delphiniums, forget-me-nots, a riot of Shasta daisies or cosmos. Borders may be uneven or permeable. Pisces have intuitive feelings about their vegetable gardens. They know without looking when the slugs are attacking the cabbage and when the beans need a drink.

The
ENVIRONMENTAL POLITICS
of the
CHRISTMAS TREE

by Ingrid Abramovitch

For those of us who are ecologically minded and have worried some about the tradition of the Christmas tree, there's reason to relax. If you bought your tree from one of the nation's 15,000 growers, you have the seal of approval from environmentalists who liken the purchase of a Christmas tree to that of a head of broccoli or any other agricultural product.

According to the National Christmas Tree Association, Christmas tree farms, which generally use land unsuitable for other kinds of crops, plant two to three trees for every tree sold. Not only do these farms discourage the pirating of trees from our forests, but they also contribute to the ecology of the region by generating oxygen and providing a habitat for birds.

But if it's okay to chop down the trees (within the farms), what about disposing of the 37 million of them that Americans buy each year? Communities across the country are coming up with innovative methods of recycling. One county in Louisiana had the National Guard drop 25,000 trees into canals in order to help restore the natural marsh vegetation. Other solutions have included weighting and sinking the trees in reservoirs to create fish habitats, using the trees to help protect the eroding shorelines or dunes, or shredding the trees for mulch. New York City alone shreds 100,000 trees each year to use for mulch in its parks and playgrounds. While detractors do say there is a limit to the amount of mulch our country needs, it is certainly a better alternative than piling the trees into our landfills.

If you live in an urban or suburban area, you can recycle your tree for your own use. Clip the branches and lay them in your garden for winter protection; rent a shredder with a group of neighbors; or chop the tree into logs, let stand a year, and use for firewood. (It is essential that you wait a year before you burn the logs to prevent releasing their creosote, a coal tar, into the atmosphere.) Or consider a live Christmas tree—but just make sure that you dig the planting hole before the ground freezes.

So next year, go ahead and enjoy your tree. But do buy from a member of the National Christmas Tree Association and ask your local sanitation or environmental department about recycling programs in your area. If they don't have such a program, your call may help spur them on.

The Perfect Present

by Elizabeth L. Haskins

With gardening fast becoming our nation's favorite pastime, you may find that more and more people on your shopping list have joined the ranks of gardening enthusiasts. Here's some help finding the perfect present next holiday season.

For the beginner gardener:
- A gardening journal. For some gardeners a beautiful blank book is perfect.
- A plant dictionary that gives both the Latin and common names.
- Bulb planter with an assortment of unusual bulbs.
- A gardening hat. Although there are many beautiful styles, it's the baseball hat my brother gave me for Christmas that I grab for when I really need to get some work done.
- Weeding basket.
- A beginner's gardening handbook. Look for one geared to their particular interests and gardening zone.

For the rosarian:
- Felco pruners (they come for lefties, too!).
- Elbow-length leather gardening gloves.
- Copper tags to identify their rosebushes.
- Rose cutter—for giving cut flowers an extra-clean cut.
- An exotic or hard-to-find rose (make sure it is climate compatible).

For the vegetable gardener:
- Vegetable-garden cookbook based on the harvest.
- Plastic owl to shoo intruders away.
- Harvesting basket.
- An assortment of colorful nasturtium seeds.
- Mesclun salad seed mix. This has been the biggest hit in my garden for three years running; it grows like crazy all season.
- Personalized recipe cards or canning labels.

For the antique lover:
- Antique botanicals. Gorgeous pages from old gardening books can often be found at antique markets or fairs and are surprisingly affordable.
- Antique lawn sprinkler. In some parts of the world, the prices are exorbitant. Keep an eye out in out-of-the-way places, flea markets, and yard sales.
- Glass cloches to warm seedlings and tender plants. The old ones are getting harder and harder to find, but if you like the old-fashioned look they bring to the garden, several garden-supply companies are offering replicas.
- Heirloom seeds for herbs and flowers. These are available from a number of seed sources.

For the organic gardener:
- Bat house. If mosquitoes are a problem, this is a great gift. A bat can consume up to 500 mosquitoes an hour.
- Book on organic pest control.
- An easy-to-assemble wooden composter.

For the animal lover:
- Hummingbird feeder. Most lovers of all creatures great and small will enjoy inviting hummingbirds to their garden.

- Squirrel feeder. For those who would rather feed these critters than shoo them away, this will keep the bushy-tailed fellows happy.
- Animal spigots for the hose.

For gardeners everywhere:
- Membership to a local botanic garden or horticultural society.
- Subscription to a gardening magazine.
- Japanese cutting scissors. Although I initially found these difficult to use, they are exquisite objects and, with a bit of practice, are useful too.
- Unusual vase or container for cut flowers.
- Sundial.
- Hand cream scented with botanic oils to soothe a gardener's chapped hands.
- Stone or cement pot—a true garden luxury.
- Torches that light up the night and keep the mosquitoes away.
- French tin flower holders. These are great for harvesting or transporting flowers, but they are beautiful enough to informally display cut flowers.
- An ornamental watering can.
- A lovely bouquet of fresh flowers—or arrange with a nearby florist to deliver at an agreed upon time throughout the year.
- A rare or unusual orchid. Who can resist the exotic beauty of such a plant? Although these can be expensive and many are stubborn about reblooming, the flowers will last a long time.

Many of the above suggestions can be found in the wide array of gardening catalogs; look also in the back of gardening magazines. But don't be afraid to use your imagination. One of my favorite gifts is a container found at the ruins of an old foundry; it looks wonderful with cut tulips.

And there are always books. If you are unsure of what your gardening friend may have, there is a new selection available in early spring and then again before Christmas. Or look for a shop that specializes in gardening books.

But what is more perfect for another gardener than a gift from your own garden? Cuttings, cut flowers, perennials divided from your own plants, or sharing the bounty of your vegetable garden is a true gift from the heart.

May the New Year

Be Happy and

Full of Worms

by Anne Raver

*L*ast weekend, on Christmas Eve, my sister asked me if I was going to take my worms to church. A friend who was going with me to hear the music at St. Thomas Episcopal Church on Fifth Avenue asked the same thing.

"No," I said. "But they have their little red bows on."

It was not such a bizarre question. I have a box of red worms in my Brooklyn kitchen composting old lettuce leaves and eggshells and such, and last October I had carried a few worm ambassadors in the procession at the Blessing of the Animals at St. John the Divine. They—and the thousands of microorganisms in their compost—rode in a painted coconut shell that I held proudly aloft as we walked up the aisle, behind the elephant and the hawk, the donkey, the chickens, the iguana, the gerbil on a satin pillow, the golden snake (which I must admit upstaged my worms a bit), and all manner of other creatures.

Hundreds of dogs barked and howled at the feet of their human friends as Paul Winter's *Missa Gaia* reached a joyful pitch, and something wild and haunting, like the call of the wolf, pierced the wonderful gloom of the great old cathedral. My heart was pounding as my worms and I were borne along on a cloud of incense, and as usual, I started to laugh—and to cry. No other form of worship touches me as deeply as this celebration, in the middle of gritty New York City, of our connection to the earth and to the animals.

So it was natural for my friends to wonder what my worms would be doing on Christmas Eve. I think people have a spiritual connection to my little red wigglers. Oh sure, some of my friends experience wormophobia. They can't stand to think of all these slimy creatures eating kitchen waste in a little dark box. It makes them think of decay, and inevitably, life. Worms are transformational. They can turn a pound of forgotten arugula and shriveled-up apples into fluffy, sweet-smelling soil. If that isn't a direct line to immortality, what is?

I was thinking about all this on Christmas morning, when I got up before dawn to start the ancestral potato rolls and fresh cranberry sauce that I was bringing to a gut-splitting feast set for four o'clock that afternoon at a friend's house on the Upper West Side.

The potato rolls come from Grandmother Moore, on my mother's side of the family, and after her death, all the women in the clan strove mightily to resurrect them. They were moist and rich from the potatoes that she simmered in the top of her double boiler every Saturday morning and then mashed in their own water before working them into the dough (which had none of those rough-hewn seven grains, mind you; just white flour, lard, salt, and a handful of white sugar).

But none of us could seem to attain the silky, heavenly texture of that bread, with its hint of potato and just the right amount of sweetness. It wasn't until Aunt Dolly went back to Grandmother's empty house and rattled about in the old pantry to find the top of the double boiler that we began to make any progress—because Grandmother's recipe said to use "just enough potatoes to fill the top of my double boiler." (Her elegant, spidery script also left the other measurements to handfuls, but that was the easy part. Somehow the potatoes are the conjurers of this masterpiece.)

Last Sunday morning, as I peeled the potatoes I'd grown this summer down in the red clay of our Maryland farm (passed down through the family on my father's side) and later worked the mashed goo into the yeasty flour with my hands, I felt all the spirits of my ancestors rise up about me, in a little kitchen in Brooklyn that looks out over water towers and television antennas and the blinking clock on top of the Watchtower building. Usually on this day, I am making bread down on the farm, where I look out on the tawny stubble of cornfields and birds flitting about in the mock orange bushes.

But I was not sad to be where I was. I was feeling the magic of something my friend Sylvia had once said. Sylvia grew up on a farm in Missouri, where wheat fields and tall silos stretch for as far as the eye can see (and where no espresso bars can be found, even in town). For 20 years, she has baked her grandmother's pies in a tiny kitchen in Greenwich Village, and when she and her companion bought a little cottage out on Long Island a few years ago, she brought lilies-of-the-valley and old roses from her great-grandmother's homestead.

"We carry the country with us, no matter where we go," Sylvia had told me one day when I was missing that Maryland clay and my dog, Molly, who is buried now on a sunny hill overlooking the fields.

I turned up Handel's *Messiah* and began to knead the dough as my mother had taught me, folding it over and pushing it down with the palms of my hands, over and over again, until the gluten in the wheat combined with air and yeast to become a living, breathing thing that pushed back with the resistance of a healthy muscle. When the dough was as satiny as a puppy's belly, I put it in my old yellow bowl and covered it as my ancestors had, with a damp cloth.

As the dough was rising, I opened up my worm box, so that the worms could hear the music better, and gave them a holiday feast of cranberries too soft for the sauce, potato peels, and anything else I could find in the bottom of my vegetable bin.

"Merry Christmas, worms," I said.

Someday I will have a dog again, and cats, and maybe even chickens if I live in the country. But right now, my red wigglers are fine pets for a city life.

And at Victor's house, where my friends and I feasted on all the treasured foods of our respective childhoods, we were surrounded by nature. Plants fill every window of Victor's old brownstone, and on his garden terrace, birds find seeds in the long grasses and berries in the shrubs and vines. After dinner, as we settled down to a little more wine and good conversation, I opened a special present from Victor—seeds of the purple asarina vine I had admired in his garden this summer and of a morning glory vine with a delicate, variegated leaf. It won't be long now before I plant them in little pots and stick them under the fluorescent lights that give my bedroom more the air of a potting shed than of a place of repose. My worms sleep there, too, by the bookshelf. But that's the way it is, on the farm in Brooklyn.

Happy New Year, worms. And keep up the good work.

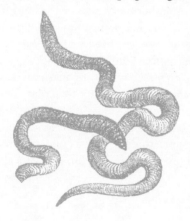

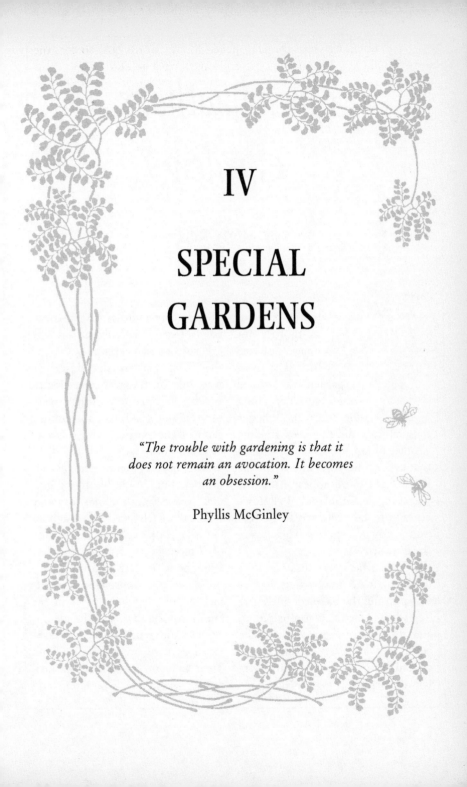

IV

SPECIAL
GARDENS

*"The trouble with gardening is that it
does not remain an avocation. It becomes
an obsession."*

Phyllis McGinley

Grandmother's Garden

by Marty Ross

It always seems as though our image of an old-fashioned garden was formed some summer long ago, in a time when hollyhocks miraculously did not need staking; peonies bloomed in such profusion that every time you cut one for the house, two more appeared on the plant; and an abundance of all flowers was to be preferred to perfection in any one species. Those were the days.

But when were they? In 1872 garden writer Anna Bartlett Warner was praising the old-fashioned garden for its "fair, rich confusion . . . and the greater the confusion, the richer." The garden, she said, should incorporate "a natural system of surprises," with plants popping up here and there in unexpected places, and in combinations with "no stiffness, no ceremony."

The garden she described was full of fragrant mignonette, roses, heliotrope, sweet peas, phloxs, and gladiolus, and among them "the little white sweet alyssum goes visiting all the day." Warner doesn't mention her grandmother, but "Grandmother's garden" is what author May Brawley Hill calls such places throughout her new book of that name, a study of American gardens of the late 19th and early 20th centuries.

Just like Impressionist painting, stories that have been in the family for decades, and the memory of an old maiden aunt, old-fashioned gardens are a bit of a blur. Their elements are charm and intimacy, fragrance, character, and good taste. Old-fashioned gardens are works of art, framed by well-kept fences, entered through gates, and ornamented with wells, urns, arbors, and the occasional, well-behaved child.

In these gardens, Latin names are banished: here thrive prince's feathers (amaranthus), lady's eardrops (fuchsia), sweet sultan (centaurea), larkspur, Jacob's ladder (valerian), foxgloves, and southernwood (artemisia). Hostas take the name our grandmothers called them, funkia lilies. Lilacs grow, naturally and conveniently, to the height of second-story windows, from which blooms may easily be gathered for great bouquets. Old-fashioned gardens are gardens of flowers, full of bees and butterflies by day and fireflies in the fading light. Of course, they represent a style, not an age, and we're still creating them today.

Unself-consciousness is an asset in any garden, but it comes partly from a conscious decision to plant at least three of everything, and let them go. It doesn't really represent an absence of planning or design but an easy relationship with nature. In an old-fashioned garden, hardy annuals are indulged in their tendency to reseed and flourish in cracks and corners the gardener hadn't thought to plant.

Old-fashioned gardens also have destinations—pergolas or patios a little removed from the house, furnished with a bench or two. These gardens make the visitor feel welcome, and allow the gardener to relax even when there is work to be done.

Timelessness is central to our idea of a "grandmother's garden," although we know that a garden is emphemeral, changing or disappearing without a trace when the garden changes hands. In an old-fashioned garden, a sundial is the only appropriate measure of time, and if the sundial happens to stand in the deep shade of an old oak, the hours will pass lightly indeed.

The Principles of
Xeriscape Gardening

by Emma Sweeney

Gardeners in the desert and semiarid regions of the United States, and in areas with a Mediterranean climate, such as southern California, have to make the best of low rainfall and prolonged drought conditions. The traditional way of coping with the dry garden is to water, but restrictions—climate, cost, conscience, even legal—mean watering is not always practical or possible. Twenty years ago, the Denver Water Board, in response to the drastic depletion of domestic water in the area, developed "xeriscaping™" which they define as "landscaping for water conservation." Today xeriscaping has gained recognition beyond Colorado and is encouraged—and indeed mandated—by utility companies in states such as Texas, Arizona, New Mexico, California, and Florida. While some utility companies mandate water usage—this is true in many parts of Texas—other water companies, including the Denver Water Department, prefer to encourage xeriscaping through education and incentives. Increased awareness in water conservation and more-stringent controls of water quality have also brought xeriscaping to more temperate regions of the United States, where utility companies and County Extension offices are educating gardeners in xeriscaping.

Xeriscaping (*xeri* means "dry" in Greek) includes seven principles to garden making: plants and design, soil improvement, minimized turf areas, plant "zones," mulches, irrigation, and maintenance.

The First Principle: Plants and design

The aim of a xeriscaped garden is a beautiful garden that is not a thirsty one. Xeriscaping makes use of indigenous plant species that require little, if any, water beyond what naturally occurs as rain or snow. To learn of xeric plants in your region, contact the water utility company in your area or the County Extension office at the local university. If you live in Colorado, write to the Denver Water Board at 1600 West 12th Ave., Denver, CO 80254. They'll provide you with a list of plants indigenous to Colorado. Some popular ornamentals (check the hardiness of each in your zone) in the xeriscaped garden include Missouri primrose (*Oenothera missouriensis*), Russian sage (*Perovskia atriplicifolia*), catmint (*Nepeta* ✕ *faassenii*), blue flax (*Linum perenne*), red valerian (*Centranthus ruber*), and purple coneflower (*Echinacea purpurea*). All of the salvias and sedums are xeric, as well as many of the campanulas and achilleas. Shrub roses tend to work well in the xeriscaped garden, in particular *Rosa* 'Sea Foam'.

Good garden design, which takes into account the topography, sun, and wind, can reduce waterings. Avoid when possible planting on top of a slope, as water naturally runs off. Make use of shaded areas, such as the north sides of buildings, and try not to plant in windy areas (when unavoidable, install windbreaks).

The Second Principle: Soil improvement

Give your garden a soil that can retain water, one that is neither too sandy nor too clayey. Sandy soils are porous, and water and nutrients drain away quickly. They should be amended with a composted manure rich in humus. Clay soils, on the other hand, are very dense and should be improved with peat moss.

The Third Principle: Minimized turf areas

Turf grasses are notoriously thirsty plants, and turf areas should be minimized. In their place, try ground covers such as snow-in-summer (*Cerastium tomentosum*) or periwinkle (*Vinca minor*). For that wide expanse of green, there's a native grass called buffalo grass (*Buchloe dacty-*

loides) that looks remarkably like lawn grass, requires very few waterings, and stays green from May to September.

The Fourth Principle: Plant "zones"
To avoid watering plants that don't need it, put thirsty plants in one area of the garden and plants that require less water in another. Take into account microclimates, making the best of naturally cool spots such as north-facing walls and shady areas.

The Fifth Principle: Mulches
Use a mulch to keep your soil cool in summer. A few good organic mulches include buckwheat hulls, shredded barks, shredded leaves, and large and small bark chips. Spread in a layer about an inch thick, these mulches help retain moisture in the soil and will, over the years, enrich it as well.

Inorganic mulches are also effective. River rocks, pea rocks, cobblestones and lava can look very attractive in the garden.

The Sixth Principle: Efficient irrigation
Drip irrigation with a soaker hose is the preferred method of watering, but it must be used properly. Any form of irrigation in a soil that cannot retain moisture is a waste. Mist sprinklers can waste water if used on rainy days, and a faulty sprinkler system (such as one that shoots water straight up) also squanders this precious resource. The key to the xeriscaped garden is to water only when absolutely necessary. Newly planted trees, shrubs, and plants need watering, and attention to new plantings is crucial to the success of the garden.

The Seventh Principle: Appropriate maintenance
Finally, the seventh principle to xeriscaping is good maintenance of the garden and of irrigation tools. This means employing good garden practices such as deadheading, cutting back, fertilizing, and weeding, as well as cleaning and maintaining sprinkler systems.

Practice these xeriscaping principles in your garden—there is a lot of good common sense here—and you'll be rewarded with strong, healthy plants in a beautiful garden.

Museum Quality Tomatoes

by Tom Armstrong

In the early 1960s, when Marcel Breuer was designing his massive modernist building for the Whitney Museum of American Art at Madison Avenue and 75th Street, he could never have imagined that one day a container vegetable garden would flourish on its fifth-floor terrace. Nor could he have imagined that the museum's director would sell the rooftop produce from a stand in front of the museum.

The 12-foot-wide terrace is a large, anonymous area, bounded by a glass wall of staff offices and tucked behind the dark granite facade he continued to the sixth floor. When I arrived as director in 1974, it was inhabited only by a number of academic, figurative sculptures by artists whose obscurity was confirmed by the placement of their work in an area closed to the public and unused by the staff.

One day it occurred to me that this outdoor space would be the ideal location for the creation of a container garden. I confided my plan to assistant director Jennifer Russell and together we began planning our garden. Soon after, the building manager joined our conspiracy and had 16 half-barrel tubs and several thousand pounds of topsoil delivered.

One weekend in early spring, when the offices were closed and no one could bother us, Jennifer and I planted the best-looking, largest, healthiest tomato plants we could find in New Jersey. Scorning our choice of "hybrids," one of the museum's electricians added a few plants he had grown from seeds obtained from a seed exchange for antique varieties.

Much to the astonishment of our colleagues, the tomato garden flourished in the hot, humid urban environment, aided by weekly doses of liquid fertilizer. Emboldened by our success, in subsequent years we added a spring crop of leaf lettuce as well as eggplants and summer annuals. In the fall we planted daffodil and tulip bulbs, which flowered throughout the next April and May.

The garden produced an abundant crop of tomatoes, which we arranged according to size on a table in my office. During our second year, it seemed appropriate to go public and share our bounty, so we set up the All-American Vegetable Stand in front of the museum.

Our emporium was open only on Tuesday evenings (also the night the museum was open late) from 6:00 to 6:30 PM. We limited the time because we had no vendors permit and were afraid that some of the neighborhood grocers might resent the competition, although our friend Billy, the hot dog vendor, encouraged us.

We displayed the tomatoes in baskets on the parapet wall surrounding the entrance to the museum, with handwritten signs indicating the price per tomato—$ 1 or $.50. We made change from a cigar box and added extras to every purchase. Our best customers were distinguished ladies who lived in the neighborhood, one of whom always arrived in a chauffeured car.

We were famous gardeners. Feature articles devoted to our garden and stand appeared in the *New York Times* and *Washington Post*. Conservative trustees complained that our endeavor was undignified. We countered by contributing all our proceeds to the annual fund, bestowing permanent recognition on the All-American Vegetable Garden as a donor of record.

We celebrated at a party where each guest wore a yellow All-American Vegetable Stand T-shirt with three bright red tomatoes emblazoned across the chest. One guest further embellished her costume, arriving as the "happy hoer."

I left the Whitney Museum in 1990 and the garden went into dormancy. The museum is currently being renovated and the fifth-floor terrace will be roofed over to create new gallery space. Soon all traces of the pleasures and rewards of a tomato garden on top of an art museum will exist only in our memories.

Carnivorous

Plants

by Eric Swanson

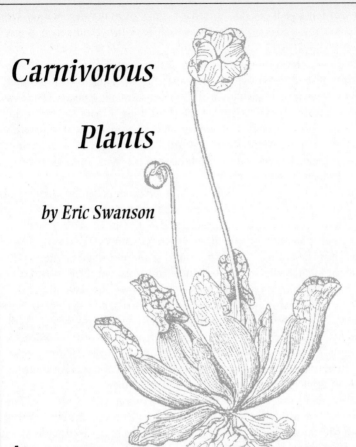

A great deal of mythology has grown up around flesh-eating plants. Unfortunately for those who may have considered these intriguing species a neat solution to the problem of garrulous relatives or obnoxious coworkers, a type that actually eats people has yet to be found. (At least, no one has ever reported finding one.) Still, nearly 450 varieties of carnivorous plants have been recorded, enough to satisfy even the most macabre sensibilities. Some are tiny fungi that subsist on a diet of unsuspecting amoebas; others are large enough to consume a lizard or a rabbit.

Common to all varieties is their unique evolutionary response to the problem of environments that do not supply sufficient nitrogen. Most varieties grow in boggy regions, where the soil is predominantly acid. Insects and other living creatures native to such regions provide a plentiful source of nitrogen, however, and through a long process of adaptation, carnivorous plants evolved the capacity to lure and trap them. Botanists have recorded three basic trap styles, which may be described as active, semiactive, and passive.

The most common example of the active type is the Venus flytrap, whose snare resembles an open clam-shaped pad ringed with pointed teeth, which lures insects inside with a delicious-smelling nectar. The first time an insect brushes against any of the three trigger hairs located inside the pad, Venus goes on alert: the soft touch may signal a meal, or merely a breath of wind. If the unlucky victim brushes the trigger a second time, both sides of the pad swing closed, and the trap fills with a liquid that first drowns and then digests its prey.

Semiactive carnivores produce leaves or flowers armed with small tendrils, whose tips secrete tiny droplets of clear, sticky fluid. The trap works in two stages. When an insect lights on a petal or brushes too close, it becomes caught in the adhesive; its ensuing struggle to escape then stimulates the tendrils to wrap around it and draw it down onto the surface of the petal, where it is drowned and digested. The most common variety of semiactive carnivores are sundews, so named because their tiny secretions shimmer in the sun. The byblis, a larger Australian species, uses the insects caught in its adhesive to lure larger prey. Attracted by what seems a ready meal, a frog or lizard is suddenly wrapped in adhesive tentacles and itself becomes a hearty main course. Not all semiactive traps possess tentacles, however. Some, like the butterwort, have sticky leaves that curl around their prey.

Pitcher plants make up the third, or passive, type of carnivores. The trap is shaped like a pitcher, with a curving sort of wing attached that is coated with nectar. A flap at the mouth of the trap is covered with small hairs that point downward into the trap itself, where more sweet-smelling juice is collected. The victim crawls easily enough down these hairs but cannot return by the same route, since the spiky tips of the hairs are too painful to travel past in reverse. The only way is down through a circle of slick hairs on which it is impossible to remain standing. Thus the victim slides into the pool of fragrant, but deadly, digestive juices. These ingenious traps vary widely in size, from tiny cups to vessels broad enough to swallow a large tropical rat.

The "Perennial" Annual Border

by Dr. Ernest T. DeMarie III

Each year millions of gardeners spend millions of dollars on millions of annuals. Our grandparents spent far less and got far more value because they chose varieties that self-sow. Many of their selections were flowers that produce seeds that drop to the ground and germinate in the spring, enabling them to maintain many annual favorites year after year.

Most of today's best-selling annual bedding plants are F_1 hybrids that are expensive to produce and often demand superior conditions for best performance. And they either form seeds that are not true—the descendants do not look exactly like the parents—or bear no seeds at all. By carefully selecting varieties that are self-sowing, the gardener can create a "perennial" annual border that can continue indefinitely as long as he or she stacks the deck:

1. Choose a sunny, well-drained part of the garden for your annual bed.
2. Avoid planting shrubs and perennials in the bed; annual seedlings resent the competition.
3. Learn to recognize small annual seedlings, so that you do not mistake them for weeds.
4. Be sure not to pull up fading annuals before their seeds have matured and dropped off.
5. Selectively remove plants with undesirable colors and any small or sickly plants.
6. Too much competition results in weaker plants; don't be afraid to thin seedlings.

The following are some favorite self-sowing annuals; one planting should provide you with flowers for years to come:

CALENDULA Sometimes called pot marigold, this orange or yellow daisy prefers cool summer nights. It may die out in the hot weather but will return in the spring. When self-sowing, plants tend to revert to hardier single-flowered forms.

CAMPION Known botanically as *Silene armeria*, this vivid pink, short-lived Mediterranean annual seeds prolifically. This resourceful plant will even resow with ease in containers and sidewalk cracks.

CLEOME Tall with airy clusters of pink or white flowers forming seedpods at the end of long stalks, cleome attracts butterflies (especially swallowtails), can grow quite large in rich soil, and makes a good cut flower.

FOUR-O'CLOCK Also known as *Mirabilis jalapa*, this big, handsome, tender South American perennial has masses of colorful flowers that open in the late afternoon. With thick carrotlike roots, it may overwinter in Zones 7 and above and forms an abundance of ornamental black seeds for self-sowing in colder zones.

IMPATIENS BALFOURI This Himalayan relative of the common impatiens is an excellent self-sower that grows over 3 feet tall and bears purple to white flowers shaped like horns of plenty dangling from the end of every branch. It will grow in part shade, tolerates any garden soil, and will readily naturalize in moist areas.

LARKSPUR This resembles a small delphinium but belongs to the genus *Consolida*. Seed sometimes germinates in the fall, forming plantlets that survive winter and grow far larger than those that come up in the spring. If the common double form is planted, the much more graceful singles will eventually appear.

NICOTIANA A tender perennial also called flowering tobacco, this will sometimes overwinter in Zones 8 and above and will resow in colder zones. Because these plants are slow to start, only in warmer zones will they flower in time to set a new crop of seed before frost.

PETUNIA INTEGRIFOLIA Although the flowers are smaller than those of the F_1 hybrids, this vigorous "old" petunia produces huge numbers of blooms and will even tolerate some frost.

POPPIES Until recently, opium poppies could be found only in older gardens, but seeds are now sold quite openly in garden centers as "peony-flowered" poppies (*Papaver somniferum*). The law-and-order crowd can look for Shirley or Flanders field poppies instead.

PORTULACA Known as moss rose, this annual succulent with brilliant single or double flowers in both pastels and shockingly bright colors requires a dry, sunny spot, free from competing tall plants, and does particularly well among rocks.

SWEET ALYSSUM Prized for its copious bloom from summer to early frost and its enchanting fragrance, this annual edging plant is a good self-sower in dry gardens.

VERBENA BONARIENSIS However beautiful this tall purple-flowered tender perennial may be, it is really just a weed and will self-sow like one, even in a perennial border. It may overwinter in Zones 8 and above, and its flowers attract butterflies.

Bear in mind that some of the most popular annuals are not reliable self-sowers, in particular: begonia, geranium (*pelargonium*), marigold (*Tagetes*), salvia (*Salvia splendens*), vinca (*Catharanthus*), and zinnia. But by knowing which varieties to plant, you can create a garden that will continue performing for years for the cost of a few seedlings or seed packets and a little yearly maintenance.

Digging It Together

by Eric Swanson

June seems to be busting out all over, as community gardens spring up across the country. Over the past 20 years, more than 500 programs have been formed nationwide to guide and advise communal gardeners. Rural residents have come together to work idle patches of farmland. Suburban dwellers have formed groups to care for public parks, beautify the grounds of local companies, or plant school gardens to teach their children that, despite claims to the contrary, ketchup is not a vegetable. Most welcome of all, urban groups such as New York City's Green Guerrillas and Operation Green Thumb, Seattle's P-Patch, SLUG (San Francisco League of Urban Gardeners), and BUG (Boston Urban Gardeners) are beating back the asphalt, turning vacant lots, sidewalks, and even rooftops into greener pastures.

Community gardens serve a variety of purposes. Some are recreational, therapeutic, or educational. Others beautify an eyesore or serve as a focus around which communities can gather to deal with larger issues, such as the isolation of the elderly, neighborhood vandalism, or youth unemployment. Some even feed the multitudes: in 1994 alone,

Philadelphia's community vegetable gardens furnished nearly $2 million worth of fruits and vegetables. Yet the main attraction of community gardening is the sheer fun of participating. It's a great way to get dirty with other people.

Unless you have a very creative imagination, the first step you'll need to take in planting a community garden is to find other interested people. Neighbors, friends, and family members as well as people you know from school, community, and church groups are all likely candidates. Once you've canvassed acquaintances, you may need to venture further afield, asking your friends to talk to people they know. You might hand out flyers, or pin them on bulletin boards in local restaurants, laundromats, and community centers. You may even try announcing an exploratory meeting in a community newspaper. Many garden groups start out informally, with leaders rising to fill needed roles; as time goes on, they organize themselves more explicitly. Some type of structure in terms of bylaws and membership fees usually ensures the stability of the group and the continuity of the garden.

Of course, it also helps to have a site for the garden. Suitability will depend on several factors. Vegetable gardens require six full hours of sunshine a day, though flower beds can manage on somewhat less. Access to water is essential, via a nearby fire hydrant (check local regulations), an agreeable neighbor's spigot, or municipal water lines running beneath or near the site. Eight to 10 inches of soil is adequate for most gardening needs, but you will need to determine its quality, as the soil may lack vital nutrients or contain toxins such as lead or copper. Many colleges and local extensions of state agricultural services provide testing for area residents. Finally, you will need to arrange for purchase or lease of the land from its rightful owner, whose identity, if unknown, can usually be determined through your local chamber of commerce.

Once you have acquired a site, it's time to get dirty. The land will have to be cleared and perhaps new soil will have to be brought in. Garden plots will need to be divided and gardening materials scrounged, begged, borrowed, or bought. If you pitch your project adroitly, you may raise funding from corporate or municipal groups such as local horticultural societies, conservation commissions, neighborhood associations, senior citizens associations, manufacturers of agricultural products, and private foundations. Don't discount schools, scout organizations, or 4-H programs: community gardens provide an extraordinary learning experience for young people, and kids involved in a garden are often its best defenders against their disaffected peers who might harbor thoughts of vandalism.

Some of the oldest community garden groups are still flourishing and will gladly share their expertise in planning, acquiring, and maintaining common plots with new groups across the country. If you see your thumbs turning green every time you pass an empty plot of land, contact any of the following organizations:

American Community Gardening Association
325 Walnut St.
Philadelphia, PA 19106-2777
(215) 625-8250
email: sallymcc@libertynet.org

Boston Urban Gardeners
46 Chestnut Ave.
Jamaica Plains, MA 02130
(617) 522-1259

Operation Green Thumb
49 Chambers St., Suite 1020
New York, NY 10007
(212) 788-8059

San Francisco League of Urban Gardeners
2088 Oakdale Ave.
San Francisco, CA 94124
(415) 285-7584

Most of these organizations can direct you to garden groups already active in your region. They can also provide information on a broad range of topics such as community composting, attracting sponsors, writing bylaws, and kids' projects. For a modest fee, many offer newsletters and training as well. The best part is, once you've collected all the information you need, community gardening becomes a simple matter of getting out, getting down, and getting dirty.

BELOVED BULBS

by Michael Ruggiero

*F*or centuries, daffodils have been associated with the coming of spring and the rejuvenation of the spirit after the dark days of winter. Never has this feeling been more evident than in Shakespeare's poem "Spring":

> When daffodils begin to peer,
> With heigh! the doxy over the dale,
> Why, then comes in the sweet o' the year,
> For the red blood reigns in the winter's pale.

The names "daffodil" and "narcissus" refer to the many beautiful cultivated and natural forms of the genus *Narcissus*. (The botanical name *Narcissus* comes from the legend of the handsome Greek youth Narcissus, who fell in love with his reflection in a pool and was transformed into a flower by the gods.) Although the common name "daffodil" refers to only a small portion of the genus (the yellow trumpet types), it has become a well-accepted common name for all types of *Narcissus*.

The daffodil's early flowering, reliability, and ease of culture make it one of the most popular spring bulbs. Most kinds are not fussy about the type of soil in which they grow as long as it is well drained. They should be planted in areas that receive sun all day long, with the exception of those varieties that have pink or deep orange cups. These types benefit from light shade during the hottest part of the day, which will prolong their flowering period and keep their colors vibrant.

After flowering, daffodils need to build up strength in order to bloom again the following year. Therefore it is very important to leave the foliage intact until it has turned brown, which usually takes about two months. If, like most people, you would prefer not to look at fading foliage, plant your bulbs among other perennials such as hostas or daylilies, whose leaves will hide the declining foliage until it can be cut back to the ground.

Daffodils should be planted as soon as they are purchased in the fall. If you cannot plant your bulbs immediately, store them in an area that is well ventilated and free from freezing temperatures or excess moisture. Avoid hot or extremely dry storage conditions, as these can, over time, damage the flower buds and even destroy the bulb.

The depth of planting is determined by the size of the bulb. The rule of thumb is to plant large bulbs with their necks 4 inches to 6 inches below the soil surface; while the necks of small bulbs should be 2 inches to 3 inches below the surface. It is always preferable to plant bulbs slightly deeper rather than too shallow.

Next year you may want to consider planting a variety of daffodils. Some of the best-loved types include:

'Accent'	White petals with large intense pink cup
'Barrett Browning'	White petals with small orange cup
'Carlton'	Two-toned yellow with large cup—the most popular daffodil
'Cassata'	White petals with ruffled lemon split cup
'Cheerfulness'	Double white flowers
'Dutch Master'	Golden yellow trumpet—often sold as King Alfred
'February Gold'	Golden cyclamineus type
'Geranium'	Three to five fragrant white and orange-cupped flowers per stem
'Ice Follies'	White petals with wide yellow cup that fades to white
'Lemon Gold'	Soft lemon-colored trumpet
'Mount Hood'	White trumpet
'Thalia'	Two to three fragrant white flowers per stem

Powerhouse Perennials

by Nicolas H. Ekstrom

*T*he ideal perennial should bloom prolifically and over a long season. In habit, or overall shape, it should be naturally attractive without much pruning or staking. Most important, it must have what is known as "good foliage"—foliage that has character even when the plant is not in bloom and that persists unblemished throughout the growing season. Free of pests and resistant to disease, our ideal perennial should be adaptable to a wide range of growing conditions and climates and thoroughly lacking in temperament. Fortunately, many perennials meet this list of high standards—more, of course, in gentle than in harsh climates. These are the plants that we can rely on to form the foundation of our flower gardens and that deserve to be called powerhouse perennials.

Achillea species—No garden should be without yarrows. The lemon yellow flowers and gray-green ferny leaves of hybrid *A.* 'Moonshine' are unsurpassed. Cultivars of *A. millefolium* are the longest bloomers and have the greatest range of colors. Zone 3.

Anthemis tinctoria—Shrubby golden marguerite exhausts itself with a continuous display of bright daisies if spent flower stems are not cut back. Numerous yellow cultivars, some white. Zone 3.

Armeria maritima—The compact little sea pinks tolerate even poor soil and seaside conditions. Masses of deep to pale pink or white flowers over delicate blue-green foliage for weeks in late spring through early summer. Zone 3.

Aster ✕ *frikartii*—One of the best of all perennials, this aster is covered with fragrant lavender-blue daisies throughout the summer and fall. Give it some winter protection in cold climates. Zone 5.

Calamintha nepeta ssp. *nepeta*—One of my special favorites, calamint is a compact plant with wonderfully aromatic foliage and a succession of tiny white or pale lilac flowers from summer to frost. Zone 5.

Centranthus ruber—Red valerian is usually bright pink, sometimes white over a bush of gray-green foliage. An easy plant that self-seeds very freely. Zone 4.

Chrysogonum virginianum—A stalwart edging plant or ground cover, native goldenstar bears yellow daisies that are rarely out of bloom. Grows in sun or partial shade. Zone 5.

Coreopsis verticillata—Thread-leaf coreopsis, truly an ideal perennial, is a well-behaved, bushy plant with delicate foliage and an endless supply of bright yellow daisies. Hybrid 'Moonbeam' has lovely pale lemon flowers. Zone 3.

Corydalis lutea—At home in either sun or shade, this relative of bleeding heart makes neat mounds of ferny foliage covered for months with yellow flowers. Zone 5.

Fragaria ✕ *frel* 'Pink Panda'—This ornamental strawberry with bright pink flowers is a charming ground cover for underplanting roses. Zone 5.

Gaillardia ✕ *grandiflora*—The lively blanketflower hybrids come in a variety of sizes and flower colors in yellow, orange, and red. Zone 3.

Geranium sanguineum var. *striatum*—This longest-blooming cranesbill bears its pink flowers with darker veins on a neat mound of pretty palmate leaves. Try *G.* 'Johnson's Blue' also. Zone 4.

Hemerocallis X *hybrida*—Many of the modern hybrid daylilies are repeaters, blooming again and again all summer long. Brassy 'Stella d'Oro' is one of the most popular, pale yellow 'Happy Returns' is even prettier; 'Fairy Tale Pink' is an award winner. Zone 3.

Kalimeris pinnatifida (syn. *Asteromoea mongolica*)—Botanists can't agree on the name, but gardeners all call this a winner. A bushy relative of asters, it is covered for months with a profusion of semidouble white flowers. Zone 5.

Lobelia siphilitica—The stately great blue lobelia is equally at home in the border and in moist spots beside streams and ponds. Cut back spent flower stalks for rebloom. Zone 4.

Malva alcea 'Fastigiata'—Tall hollyhock mallow displays its large pink flowers at the back of the border all summer long. Zone 4.

Malva moschata—Shorter and bushier, the airier musk mallow comes in both pink and white. Self-seeds with abandon. Zone 3.

Nepeta X *faassenii*—Best close up, catmint's lovely gray foliage and lavender flowers make it an excellent edging plant. Cut back by half for rebloom. Zone 3.

Phlox paniculata—Look for the new mildew-resistant cultivars of the stately summer phlox. Not completely trouble-free, but worth the extra effort. Many colors. Zone 3.

Platycodon grandiflorus—Blue, pink, or white flowers beloved by children top the straight stems of balloon flower. Deadhead for neatness. Zone 3.

Rudbeckia fulgida var. *sullivantii* 'Goldsturm'—The orange coneflower makes a big bushy plant covered with black-eyed Susans all summer. Zone 3.

Scabiosa columbaria 'Butterfly Blue'—A recent addition to the gardener's palette, this neat, graceful plant bears masses of lavender-blue 2-inch flower heads from May to November. 'Pink Mist' is even newer. Zone 5.

Stokesia laevis—Stokes' asters are ideal long-blooming perennials for the front of the border. Many cultivars with large 4-inch flower heads in white, pink, blue, and yellow. Zone 5.

Veronica species—There are so many good speedwells that it is hard to choose among them. Sturdy 'Sunny Border Blue' has dark violet-blue spikes from June to frost. *V. spicata* 'Icicle' bears white spikes all summer.

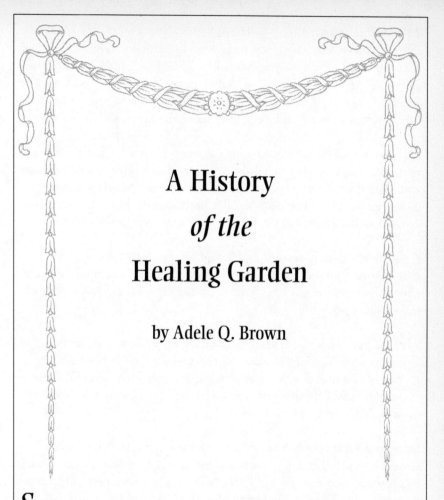

A History
of the
Healing Garden

by Adele Q. Brown

Savory herbs in a kitchen garden not only add zest to meals, but in times of yore they were the basis of many homemade medicines. The leaves, bark, berries, roots, and flowers of the garden were, no doubt, tried and tested on many, weary subjects through the centuries. Surely as much suffering was engendered as was alleviated.

Nevertheless, these folksy experiments produced much heralded claims about cures for a myriad of ills. This lore has become a rich part of our heritage. But lore, simply put, is a kernel of truth wrapped in a mystery that has been passed down through generations. Of course, *none of these uses is recommended*. If you are serious about a plant's actual healing properties, seek guidance from a medical professional.

In the Backyard:

Basil (*Ocimum basilicum*), was thought to have supernatural powers, and people prayed to it as a guardian spirit. Found in Hindu and Egyptian tombs, basil was believed to help transport the deceased to the Afterworld. After learning about its purported relaxing properties, our forefathers employed basil to quiet epilepsy, dizziness, and insomnia.

Rosemary (*Rosmarinus officinalis*) has been eaten with salt to improve eyesight, drunk as wine to aid digestion, used as a salve to heal wounds, and infused with compresses to relieve stiff joints. There is practically no complaint to which rosemary has not been applied; blossoms were even candied and consumed in the 14th century to thwart the Black Death.

Dandelion (*Taraxacum officinale*) sap was said to cure eye diseases, rheumatism, jaundice, and circulation difficulties. Country lore maintained that rubbing one's body in the white sap of the dandelion would make your wishes come true.

Sage (*Salvia officinalis*) is associated with both wisdom and fertility. The herb was used in salves, tonics, and teas and reportedly helped relieve a myriad of complaints ranging from vertigo to gum inflammation, asthma, and muscle aches. To disinfect sickrooms, sage leaves were slowly burned in an open fire or boiled in a pot.

Sweet marjoram (*Origanum majorana*) is associated with happiness. The Greeks believed that if marjoram bloomed on a grave, the deceased would be propelled into eternal bliss. In the Middle Ages, marjoram was an antidote to a witch's spells. American colonists used it for bronchitis, coughs, migraines, insomnia, stomach and liver disorders, and rheumatism and as a form of medicinal snuff.

Thyme (*Thymus vulgaris*) was used by the Egyptians, Greeks, and Etruscans as a perfume, cosmetic, and embalming herb. Medieval folklore equated the herb with courage because knights carried sprigs cut by their sweethearts into battle. European settlers carried their thyme-based remedies for insomnia, anemia, and colds to America. Once here, thyme was applied to the scalp as a tonic to prevent hair loss. And, like marjoram, it was used as snuff to relieve congestion.

In the Meadow:

In addition to the common, savory herbs, there are hundreds that grow wild as they did in the 17th and 18th centuries.

Blackberry (*Rubus fructicosus*) berries were used as a gargle for sore throats. They were also thought to cure loose teeth and protruding eyes. Early on it was discovered that crushed blackberry leaves stopped the bleeding of the very cuts made by its thorny canes.

Chicory (*Cichorium intybus*) root is well known as a substitute for coffee. A chicory root and alcohol massage was said to arrest withering limbs. In other forms it was thought to clean the blood and cure anemia, arthritis, constipation, and dropsy.

Dandelion (*Taraxacum officinale*) sap was said to cure eye diseases, rheumatism, jaundice, and circulation difficulties. Country lore maintained that rubbing one's body in the white sap of the dandelion would make your wishes come true.

In the Arbor:

The abundance of trees in North America was a boon to home herbalists. Early settlers brought their European superstitions and remedies across the Atlantic, but they then learned about indigenous trees from Native Americans. "Waste not, want not": family practitioners considered all parts of a tree as potential sources of alimentary benefit.

Ash (*Fraxinus*) trees were used to cure cattle with sore limbs.

The aches were thought to be caused by tiny shrews running over the sleeping beasts. Legend reports that a shrew was stuffed in a hole of an ash tree, the hole was plugged, and the tree thereafter was known as a "shrew ash." One touch of its branch purportedly cured the cattle's soreness for good

Supernatural powers were also attributed to ash trees. To determine a sick child's fate, the ailing infant would be passed three or four times through the opening of a freshly split sapling, then the tree would be bandaged back together. If the tree survived, so would the child; a dead tree augured poorly for the infant.

Birch (*Betula alba*) was seen as providing medicinal benefits even though its fine branches were sometimes used as switches to punish misbehavior. The sap of the tree, "birch blood" or "birch water," was valued for healing skin diseases and rheumatism.

Dogwood (*Cornus*) trees have a bitter bark that was made into a tea by Native Americans to help reduce fevers. Pioneers used dogwood against malaria, and during the Civil War, Southerners, short on quinine, drank a dogwood concoction as a medicinal substitute.

Elder (*Sambucus*) shrubs were known not only for the sweet wine their berries produced but also for infusions that, depending on the exact proportions of buds, leaves, and fruit, purportedly cured insomnia, reduced fever, or prolonged one's life. A wreath of elder leaves around a horse's neck did not signify a champion—it was employed merely to repulse flies.

Elm (*Ulmus fulva*) twigs were tied to milking buckets to improve the consistancy of butter. Native Americans taught colonists how to get nourishment from the sticky inner bark of the slippery elm, which was later used as a tonic for coughs and as a dressing for boils.

RATING AMERICA'S BEST BOTANIC GARDENS

by Thomas Cooper

Rating: ❀ (lowest) ❀❀❀❀❀ (best)

Berkeley Botanical Garden
University of California
Centennial Dr.
Berkeley, CA 94720
Hours: 9 A.M.–4:45 P.M.
Size: 32 acres
Gardens:
perennials ❀❀❀❀
herbs ❀❀❀
Greenhouses/conservatories ❀❀
Special Features: An extensive collection of mature trees and shrubs. Many plants native to the region, plus plants from New Zealand, Australia, South Africa, and South America. Good views across the Bay.

Boyce Thompson Southwestern Arboretum
37615 Highway 60
Superior, AZ 85273
Hours: 8 A.M.–5 P.M. (except Dec. 25)
Size: 1,076 acres
Gardens:
perennials ❀❀❀
herbs ❀❀
Greenhouses/conservatories ❀❀
Teaching gardens ❀❀❀
Special Features: Extensive plantings of cacti and succulents. Spring rains spur extravagant flowering of annuals and perennials. Good armadillo watching.

Brooklyn Botanic Garden
1000 Washington Ave.
Brooklyn, NY 11225
Hours: Tue.–Fri., 8 A.M.–4:30
P.M.; Sat.–Sun. 10 A.M.–4:30 P.M.
Size: 50 acres
Gardens:
perennials ❀❀❀
roses ❀❀❀
water ❀❀
herbs ❀❀❀
Japanese ❀❀
Greenhouses/conservatories ❀❀
Woodlands ❀❀❀
Rock gardens ❀❀❀
Vegetable/fruit ❀❀
Teaching gardens ❀❀❀
Special Features: The Cranford Rose Garden is an extensive, beautifully grown collection of old and modern roses. There is a garden for the blind designed by Alice Ireys. The crab apples and cherries make a stunning spring display. In fall, the traditional techniques of training chrysanthemums are on display at the Chrysanthemum Festival.

Chicago Botanical Gardens
1000 Lake Cook Rd.
Glencoe, IL 60022
(847) 835-5440
Hours: 8 A.M.–Sunset
Size: 300 acres
Gardens:
perennials ❀❀❀
roses ❀❀❀
water ❀❀❀
herbs ❀❀❀
Japanese ❀❀❀
Greenhouses/conservatories ❀❀❀
Woodlands ❀❀
Rock gardens ❀❀
Vegetable/fruit ❀❀
Teaching gardens ❀❀❀
Special Features: Good collections of native plants. A prairie garden; strong fruit and vegetable teaching gardens. Japanese garden stretches over a collection of small ponds.

Dumbarton Oaks
1703 32nd St., N.W.
Washington, DC 20007
(202) 339-6450
Hours: Tue.–Sat., 2 P.M.–5 P.M.
Size: 16 (expensive) acres
Gardens:
perennials ❀❀❀
roses ❀❀
water ❀❀❀
herbs ❀❀
Japanese
Greenhouses/conservatories ❀❀
Woodlands ❀❀❀
Special Features: A beautiful and rare example of landscape of ameri-

can architect Beatrix Farrand's design, with numerous theme gardens. Massive trees. Elegant, ingenious hedges, walls, and walks.

Fairchild Tropical Garden

10901 Old Cutler Rd.
Miami, FL 33156
(305) 667-1651
Hours: 9:30 A.M.–4:30 P.M.
Size: 83 acres
Gardens:
perennials ✾✾✾
water ✾✾✾✾
Greenhouses/conservatories ✾✾✾✾
Rock gardens ✾✾✾
Special Features: Laid out by landscape designer W. L. Phillips, a disciple of Frederick Law Olmsted. Special collection of orchids, ferns, bromeliads. World's largest collection of palms. Keep an eye out for alligators on the prowl.

Filoli

Canada Rd.
Woodside, CA 94062
(415) 364-8300
Hours: Feb. 18–Nov. 1;
Tue.–Thur., reservations required;
Fri.–Sat., 10 A.M.–2 P.M.
Size: 17 acres
Gardens:
perennials ✾✾✾
roses ✾✾
water ✾✾
herbs ✾✾✾
Woodlands ✾✾
Special Features: A stunning formal

layout—site of the opening shots for the television show *Dynasty.* The Camperdown elms and tightly trimmed olives are magnificent at any season. Richly colored formal bedding schemes are dramatic, as are the red and gray borders.

Huntington Botanical Garden

1151 Oxford Rd.
San Marino, CA 91108
(818) 405-2141
Hours: Tues.–Fri., 12–4:30 P.M.;
Sat.–Sun., 10:30 A.M.–4:30 P.M.
Size: 207 acres
Gardens:
perennials ✾✾✾✾✾
roses ✾✾✾✾
water ✾✾✾
herbs ✾✾✾
Japanese ✾✾✾✾
Rock gardens ✾✾✾
Special Features: Ten acres of cacti and succulents; 1,500 camellias. Japanese, Shakespeare, and rose gardens, among others.

Longwood Gardens

Kennett Square, PA 19348
(610) 388-6741
Hours: 9 A.M.–6 P.M.
Size: 700 acres
Gardens:
perennials ❀❀❀❀
roses ❀❀❀❀
water ❀❀❀❀
herbs ❀❀❀❀
Japanese
Greenhouses/conservatories ❀❀❀❀❀
Woodlands ❀❀❀
Rock gardens ❀❀❀❀
Vegetable/fruit ❀❀❀❀
Teaching gardens ❀❀❀❀❀
Special Features: Outstanding conservatories 4 acres under glass.(see the silver garden designed by Isabelle Greene). Numerous theme gardens. Water water everywhere, with fountains galore, and illuminated fountain displays on summer evenings.

Marie Selby Botanical Garden

811 S. Palm Ave.
Sarasota, FL 34236
Hours: 10 A.M.–5 P.M. (except Dec. 25)
Size: 7 acres
Gardens:
perennials ❀❀❀❀
water ❀❀❀
Greenhouses/conservatories ❀❀❀❀
Woodlands ❀❀❀
Vegetable/fruit ❀❀❀❀
Teaching gardens ❀❀❀
Special Features: Trees hung with epiphytes (orchids, ferns, bromeliads). Greenhouses home to a wide array of orchids, many rare. Tropical fruits and vegetables in test garden.

New York Botanical Garden

200th St. and Southern Boulevard
Bronx, NY 10458
Hours: Tue.–Sun., 10 A.M.–4 P.M.
Size: 250 acres
Gardens:
perennials ❀❀❀
roses ❀❀❀
water ❀❀❀
herbs ❀❀❀
Japanese ❀❀❀
Greenhouses/conservatories ❀❀❀❀
Woodlands ❀❀❀
Rock gardens ❀❀❀❀
Vegetable/fruit ❀❀❀
Teaching gardens ❀❀❀❀
Special Features: Theme gardens of every sort, from alpines to woodlands. The Enid Haupt conservatory, recently refurbished, houses a great collection of tropical and otherwise tender plants.

North Carolina State University Botanical Garden

NCSU Arboretum
Dept. of Horticultural Science
North Carolina State University
Box 7609
Raleigh, NC 27695
(919) 515-3132
Hours: 8 A.M.–dusk
Size: 8 acres

Gardens:
perennials ✿✿✿✿
roses ✿✿
water ✿✿
herbs ✿✿
Vegetable/fruit ✿✿
Teaching gardens ✿✿✿✿
Special Features: An exhaustive and stunning display of interesting plants from the southern garden. The magnificent 300-foot-long perennial border proves there is more to gardening in the South than tractor tires filled with marigolds.

Pacific Tropical Botanical Gardens

P.O. Box 340
Lawai, HI 96765
(808) 332-7361
Hours: Call for hours
Size: 186 acres
Gardens:
perennials ✿✿✿✿
Woodlands ✿✿✿✿
Fruits and vegetables ✿✿✿✿
Special Features: An extensive collection of tropical plants—including Hawaiian natives—in a lush naturalistic setting.

Strybing Arboretum

Golden Gate Park
9th Avenue and Lincoln Way
San Francisco, CA 94122
(415) 661-1316
Hours: Weekdays, 8:30–4:30; Weekends and Holidays, 10 A.M.–5 P.M.
Size: 75 acres (with adjacent Japanese garden)
Gardens:
perennials ✿✿✿✿
roses ✿✿✿
water ✿✿✿
herbs ✿✿✿✿
Japanese ✿✿✿✿
Greenhouses/conservatories ✿✿✿
Woodlands ✿✿✿✿
Rock gardens ✿✿✿✿
Teaching gardens ✿✿✿
Special Features: Great displays of plants from South Africa, New Zealand, Australia, and the Himalaya. The meadow garden uses native plants to get the effects of water without the water. The fragrant garden for the blind appeals to all.

U.S. Botanic Garden

Maryland Avenue, S.W.
Washington, D.C. 20024
(202) 225-8333
Hours: 9 A.M.–5 P.M.
Size: 5½ acres open to the public.
Gardens:
perennials ✿✿✿
roses ✿✿✿
water ✿✿✿
herbs ✿✿✿
Greenhouses/conservatories ✿✿✿✿
Special Features: Situated just below the Capitol, the oldest botanic garden in the United States is a delightful respite from politics. Striking containers out-

side in summer, with adjacent rose garden. Indoor gardens range from tropics to desert, with an emphasis on the history and economic value of plants.

U.S. National Arboretum
3501 New York Ave., N.E.
Washington, DC 20002
(202) 245-2726
Hours: 8 A.M.–5 P.M. (except Dec. 25)
Size: 444 acres
Gardens:
perennials ❀❀❀
roses ❀❀❀
water ❀❀❀
herbs ❀❀❀❀
Japanese ❀❀❀❀
Greenhouses/conservatories ❀❀❀
Woodlands ❀❀❀❀
Rock gardens ❀❀❀
Teaching gardens ❀❀❀❀
Special Features: Many collections of trees and shrubs, notably the Morrison Azalea collection, the Gotelli Conifer collection, and the National Bonsai collection. Also 2 acres of herb displays.

Wave Hill
675 W. 252 St.
Bronx, NY 10471
Hours: Tue.–Sun., 9 A.M.–4:30 P.M.

Size: 28 acres
Gardens:
perennials ❀❀❀❀❀
water garden ❀❀❀❀
herb gardens ❀❀❀
Greenhouses/conservatories ❀❀❀❀
Woodland garden ❀❀❀❀
Special Features: An extraordinary range of hardy and tender plants, brilliantly arranged. Superb containers. Great winter displays in the conservatory. The views across the Hudson River to the Palisades are alone worth the visit.

Winterthur
Winterthur, DE 19735
(302) 888-4600
Hours: Mon.–Sat., 9 A.M.–5 P.M.; Sun., 12–5 P.M.
Size: 60 acres
Gardens:
perennials ❀❀❀
water ❀❀❀
Woodlands ❀❀❀❀❀
Rock gardens ❀❀❀
Special Features: One of the finest spring displays—azaleas, rhododendrons, bulbs—in the country. A glorious naturalistic design. The former Du Pont house is packed—nay, jammed—with Early American antiques.

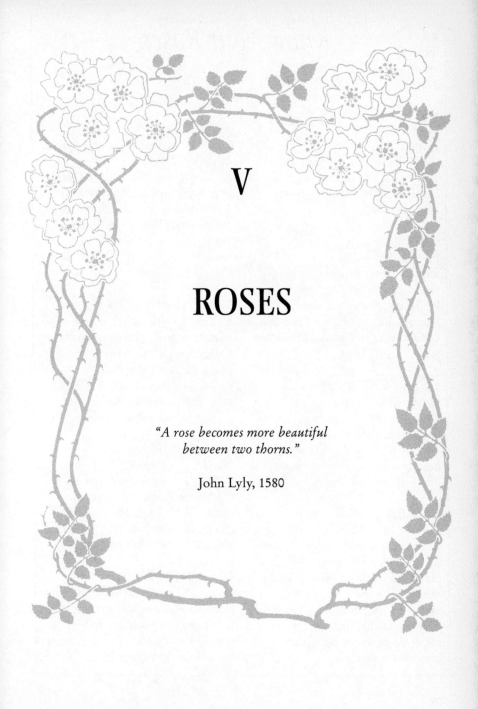

V

ROSES

*"A rose becomes more beautiful
between two thorns."*

John Lyly, 1580

Know Your Roses

by Peter C. Jones

HYBRID TEAS
Height: 3 to 5 feet;
the Rolls Royce of roses, lots of
class but a bit staid; flowers are
large, beautifully proportioned,
and fragrant.

GRANDIFLORA
Height: 5 to 8 feet;
a Caddy limo that can closely
resemble a hybrid tea; flowers are
borne on long stems, singly or in
clusters; like your limo, they add a
certain je ne sais quoi to the drive-
way.

FLORIBUNDAS
Height: 2 to 3 feet;
a Beamer known for its neat, compact habit; these roses are borne in
clusters of several to many flowers;
built low to the ground, they corner well in low borders.

CLIMBING ROSES
Height: 10 to 30 feet;
a Porsche for social-climbing gardeners seeking an impressive display with vigorous growth and
season-long color; the relentlessly
upwardly mobile will be amazed
to discover that like their motor-
car, these roses are more than a
mere status symbol.

RAMBLERS
Height: 10 to 40 feet with a spread
of up to 50 feet;
no longer manufactured in Detroit,
in part because it's usually a no-
repeat bloomer; these classic arching roses ramble in large trees
(such as apple trees) or cover
unsightly buildings (such as your
neighbor's house).

MINIATURE ROSES
Height: 6 to 18 inches; unlike
miniature golf, where you get the
green but not the fairway, this
perky Honda Civic is in all
respects (foliage, buds, flowers) a
pint-size version of larger roses,
perfect for miniature gardens.

SHRUB ROSES
Height: 2 to 9 feet;
a Ford Bronco; known as roses for
the masses, these are sometimes
called Clinton roses because they
can grow as wide as they are tall
and are useful when hedging.

GROUND-COVER ROSES
Height: 12 to 18 inches; a Mustang
known for dense, low growth that
is designed to prevent yupsters
who like to hit the ground running
from doing so in bare feet.

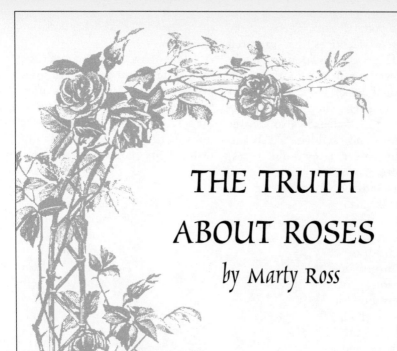

THE TRUTH ABOUT ROSES

by Marty Ross

*E*verything you've ever heard about roses is true. Some roses are easy to grow, others are finicky beyond belief; there are hardy roses and those that can't stand a frost; some tolerate bugs and blights, others seem to succumb to even the suggestion of infestation or disease. Many roses contribute generously to the garden's character, with attractive foliage, copious bloom, and shiny red or orange hips; others are glorious in bloom but disappear into the landscape as the flowers fade.

Nearly every gardener has an opinion or two, which makes it hard to keep the facts straight. For the love of a rose, some gardeners are willing to spray, coddle, prune, and pamper. Tough gardeners demand tough roses and ruthlessly weed out those that need too much care.

Rose fashions come and go. Beginners often choose hybrid teas, such as 'Tiffany', 'Chrysler Imperial', and 'Peace', graceful long-stemmed roses with voluptuous pointed buds. These are the postwar valentines that captured the fancy of a nation suddenly endowed with leisure time and plenty of pocket money.

Garden shops and mail-order specialists also offer climbers and ramblers, shrub and ground-cover roses, old roses, miniatures, roses trained into the form of small trees, flori-bundas, grandifloras, and a growing selection of modern English roses, which combine the fragrance and character of old roses with disease resis-tance and hardiness.

Roses have been around for 30 million years, but the glossy catalogs that come in the mail every spring inform us that hybridizers are not quite finished with the business of perfecting the rose: there are about 100 species and thousands of hybrid varieties. No single rose is really right for every gardener, and love of one rose seldom precludes passion for another. You rarely meet a gardener who has just one rosebush.

Before you commit to a rose, look around your garden. All roses need sun; four hours a day is often regarded the minimum, but unless they receive six, your roses are unlikely to become the beautifully lush plants you may imagine. Roses must have well-drained soil deep enough to accommodate their roots and rich enough to help them achieve their real potential. In a climate with piercingly cold winters, choose hardy roses that can tolerate low temperatures without too much special pro-tection. Warm-climate garden-ers need roses that resist the diseases encouraged by long, hot summers.

Visit rose gardens in your area, and take notes on pleasing varieties. Every rose has a person-ality, but most roses behave slightly differently in every gar-den and for every gardener. Once you find the right roses for your garden, climate, and conditions, they will shrug off occasional problems and make you look like an expert.

Don't get stuck in a relationship with roses you don't really care for: it may take time to find the right ones, and no one should imagine that it will be easier than any of the other fine things in life. Even "easy" roses are not completely carefree. Regular, deep watering and the judicious use of fertilizers are practically essential.

In your own garden, plant a rose or two at a time, and add more as the garden grows and its character develops. Dig a good, large hole when you plant, and dote a bit on newly planted roses until they settle in. The simple truth is, once they do, you'll wonder how you ever imagined a garden without them.

In Search of the Perfect Rose

by Virginia Devlin

Defining the perfect rose would be a difficult task—just ask a group of rose gardeners for their opinion on the subject! Red, yellow, pink. Hybrid tea, floribunda, climber. Flower form, fragrance, foliage. The possibilities are endless.

While perfection may allude us, exceptional garden roses receive notoriety through the All-America Rose Selection Trials. Since 1938, this nonprofit association of rose producers and introducers has evaluated new rose hybrids in a quest to find the best of the best for American gardeners.

Of the hundreds of roses introduced each year, only a handful earn the AARS distinction. Winners are selected upon completion of a rigorous two-year testing process conducted in 22 trial gardens throughout the United States. Roses are given the same care an average gardener would provide and are evaluated twice yearly by highly trained AARS judges. The roses are scored from poor to excellent in each of 15 categories, including flower form, color, fragrance, foliage, and disease resistance.

Through the years thousands of roses have competed for the AARS title. As of 1997, only 159 have succeeded, including classics like 'Double Delight' (1977), 'Mr. Lincoln' (1965), 'Peace' (1946), 'Tropicana' (1963) and 'Queen Elizabeth' (1955). The 1997 winners are 'Artistry', a coral-orange hybrid tea; 'Timeless', a deep rose-pink hybrid tea; and Scentimental', a burgundy-and-cream-striped floribunda. 'Scentimental' is the first striped rose to win the AARS award.

The TRIUMPH of "PEACE"

The story of the 'Peace' rose is as astonishing as the rose itself. In 1939 the distinguished French nurseryman Francis Meilland discovered a promising new rose nurtured from a single seed. With the dark clouds of World War II threatening the flower's fate, Meilland dispatched cuttings of the rose to growers in Italy, Germany, and the United States, including Pennsylvania grower Robert Pyle.

As tanks plowed the earth around Lyons, Pyle's precious package was slipped aboard the last plane out before the Nazis occupied France. But it would be four years before Meilland received word of his hybrid's fate. "My eyes are fixed in fascinated admiration on a glorious rose," Pyle wrote. "Its pale gold, cream and ivory petals blend into a lightly ruffled edge of delicate carmine. I am convinced that it will be the greatest rose of the century."

The rose was called 'Peace' and its beauty was enhanced in 1945 by the drama surrounding its public introduction. A flurry of doves marked the official christening at the Pacific Rose Society's spring show, while halfway around the world Allied forces claimed Berlin. On May 8 each of the original United Nations delegates was presented with a 'Peace' rose and a message of world harmony. And on August 15, as newspapers trumpeted Japan's surrender, 'Peace' received the All-American Rose Selections award of honor.

A decade later more than 30 million 'Peace' rosebushes bloomed worldwide. Meilland marveled at the miracle of his hybrid tea, saying, "How strange to think that these millions of rosebushes sprang from a tiny seed no bigger than the head of a pin, a seed we might so easily have overlooked or neglected in a moment of inattention."

ALL - AMERICA

1940
Dickson's Red
Flash
The Chief
World's Fair

1941
Apricot Queen
California
Charlotte Armstrong

1942
Heart's Desire

1943
Grande Duchesse
   Charlotte
Mary Margaret McBride

1944
Fred Edmunds
Katherine T. Marshall
Lowell Thomas
Mme. Chiang Kai-shek
Mme. Marie Curie

1945
Floradora
Horace McFarland
Mirandy

1946
Peace

1947
Rubaiyat

1948
Diamond Jubilee
High Noon
Nocturne
Pinkie
San Fernando
Taffeta

1949
Forty-niner
Tallyho

1950
Capistrano
Fashion
Mission Bells
Sutter's Gold

1951
No selection

1952
Fred Howard
Helen Traubel
Vogue

1953
Chrysler Imperial
Ma Perkins

1954
Lilibet
Mojave

1955
Jiminy Cricket
Queen Elizabeth
Tiffany

1956
Circus

1957
Golden Showers
White Bouquet

1958
Fusilier
Gold Cup
White Knight

1959
Ivory Fashion
Starfire

1960
Fire King
Garden Party
Sarabande

1961
Duet
Pink Parfait

1962
Christian Dior
Golden Slippers
John S. Armstrong
King's Ransom

1963
Royal Highness
Tropicana

1964
Granada
Saratoga

1965
Camelot
Mister Lincoln

1966
American Heritage
Apricot Nectar
Matterhorn

1967
Bewitched
Gay Princess
Lucky Lady
Roman Holiday

1968
Europeana
Miss All-American
   Beauty
Scarlet Knight

1969
Angel Face

R O S E   S E L E C T I O N S

Comanche
Gene Boerner
Pascali

1970
First Prize

1971
Aquarius
Command Performance
Redgold

1972
Apollo
Portrait

1973
Electron
Gypsy
Medallion

1974
Bahia
Bon Bon
Perfume Delight

1975
Arizona
Oregold
Rose Parade

1976
America
Cathedral
Seashell
Yankee Doodle

1977
Double Delight
First Edition
Prominent

1978
Charisma
Color Magic

1979
Friendship
Paradise
Sundowner

1980
Cherish
Honor
Love

1981
Bing Crosby
Marina
White Lightnin'

1982
Brandy
French Lace
Mon Cheri
Shreveport

1983
Sun Flare
Sweet Surrender

1984
Impatient
Intrigue
Olympiad

1985
Showbiz

1986
Broadway
Touch of Class
Voodoo

1987
Meidomonac (Bonica '82)
New Year
Sheer Bliss

1988
Amber Queen
Mikado
Prima Donna

1989
Class Act
Debut
New Beginning
Tournament of Roses

1990
Pleasure

1991
Carefree Wonder
Perfect Moment
Sheer Elegance
Shining Hour

1992
All That Jazz
Brigadoon
Pride 'n Joy

1993
Child's Play
Rio Samba
Solitude
Sweet Inspiration

1994
Caribbean
Midas Touch
Secret

1995
Brass Band
MACIvy (Singin' In
   The Rain)

1996
Carefree Delight
Livin' Easy
Mt. Hood
St. Patrick

1997
Artistry
Scentimental
Timeless

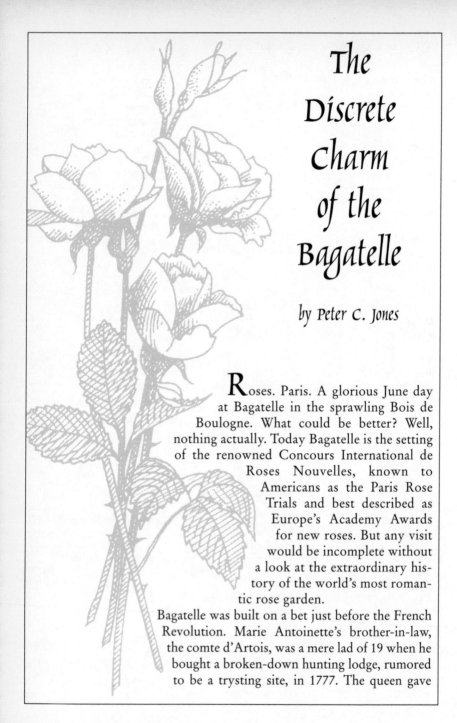

The Discrete Charm of the Bagatelle

by Peter C. Jones

Roses. Paris. A glorious June day at Bagatelle in the sprawling Bois de Boulogne. What could be better? Well, nothing actually. Today Bagatelle is the setting of the renowned Concours International de Roses Nouvelles, known to Americans as the Paris Rose Trials and best described as Europe's Academy Awards for new roses. But any visit would be incomplete without a look at the extraordinary history of the world's most romantic rose garden.

Bagatelle was built on a bet just before the French Revolution. Marie Antoinette's brother-in-law, the comte d'Artois, was a mere lad of 19 when he bought a broken-down hunting lodge, rumored to be a trysting site, in 1777. The queen gave what is now Bagatelle one glance and made him a "heads I win, tails you lose" proposition, wagering the staggering sum of 100,000 livres that he couldn't erect a new house in 60 days.

That was apparently the kind of challenge that profligate French aristocrats couldn't resist. Nine hundred men worked around the clock under the direction of François Josef Belanger, the last of the big-league ancien régime architects, and delivered the storybook château on time at the ultimate cost of 2 million livres. Marie Antoinette saw the completion of the garden in 1786, seven years before she herself was deadheaded in 1793.

Bagatelle suffered little damage during the Revolution and fell into the hands of immensely rich English Francofiles. The last of these, Richard Wallace, left it to his widow, who left it to her immensely fat male secretary, who was in love with Lady Sackville, who sired Vita Sackville-West, who recalled hanging garlands on the stone nymphs in the grottoes.

The gelatinous secretary ultimately sold Bagatelle to the city of Paris in 1905, and construction was begun on the present rose garden, designed by landscape architect J. C. N. Forestier. From the outset Bagatelle was devoted to the cultivation of modern roses, and the Rose Trials began in 1907. Not even world wars have interrupted them and the serious work of their judges.

Bagatelle on the morning of the Rose Trials is every gardener's dream come true. The jurors approach through a long, dark, verdant tunnel, lit at the end by the l'Orangerie exploding in the sunlight. In the distance lies the rose garden at peak bloom, a Monet-esque fantasy, with Empress Eugénie's hillside Chinese pavilion still slightly shrouded by the morning mist.

Hats are everywhere. Freshly creased linens stroll among the tables. Fine silks flutter in the gentle breeze. Nervous breeders, there to observe, wear suits so new that the jacket pockets are still stitched shut. With the "technical marks" already compiled by the Permanent Commission and the garden staff, the jurors set to work to heroic music. Bend and sniff (but no scratching!) is the order of the day as the judges literally beat around the bushes.

The awards are presented in the l'Orangerie from a stage surrounded by topiary columns and festooned with roses. The director of the Bois de Boulogne holds each rose aloft as the breeders step up to claim their prizes. But the serious business of judging roses cannot stay serious forever. Outside in the golden afternoon light, private-label Bagatelle champagne is flowing.

Stephen Scanniello's Top Ten

Stephen Scanniello, curator of the Cranford Rose Garden at the Brooklyn Botanic Garden, has represented the United States at the Paris Rose Trials (the Concours International de Roses Nouvelles) for many years. Here are his favorite Bagatelle gold medal winners:

1976 'Grand Siècle' France, pink hybrid tea, available in the United States under the name 'Great Century'

1974 'Matangi' Ireland, fiery red floribuna

1960 'Clair Matin' France, semidouble blush climber

1959 'Garden Party' United States, white hybrid tea

1954 'Mojave' United States, orange hybrid tea

1951 'Confidence' France, pink hybrid tea

1949 'Fashion' United States, coral floribunda

1936 'Eclipse' United States, yellow hybrid tea

1932 'Mme. Cochet-Cochet France, apricot hybrid tea

1927 'Mme. Gregoire Staechelin' France, pink climber; beautiful display at New York's Wave Hill

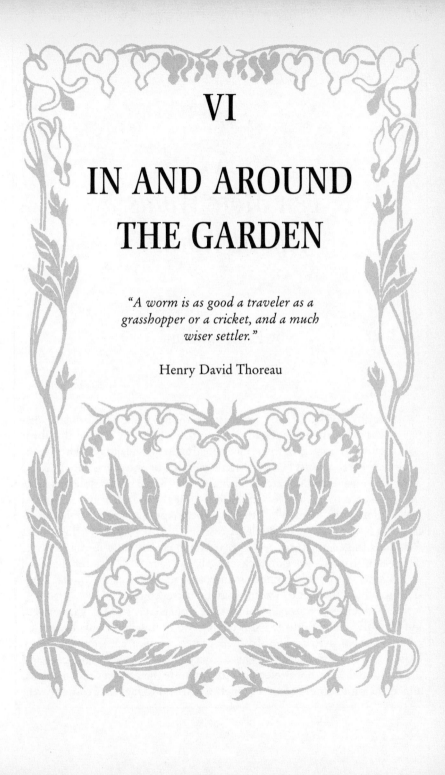

VI

IN AND AROUND
THE GARDEN

"A worm is as good a traveler as a grasshopper or a cricket, and a much wiser settler."

Henry David Thoreau

A
Few More Words About Worms

by Eric Swanson

ealthy soil contains a great many things that should not be discussed at the table. Gardening texts try to work around this difficulty by referring to certain constituents of healthy soil as organisms—a term that must be enunciated carefully, or else one is sure to cause a stir. Organisms can be categorized as either visible or invisible. Invisible organisms are by far the less exasperating of the two, because the naked eye cannot detect them, while the unpleasant appearance of visible organisms tends to upset most people. A case in point is Annelida Oligochaeta ("hairless ringed creatures"), which are often cruelly described as worms. This is unfortunate, since oligochaetes play a crucial role in nourishing the soil, whereas one could point to many other members of the animal kingdom to whom the name "worm" may be better suited.

Oligochaetes normally inhabit the upper layers of the garden bed, but they dig deeply into the soil during the hottest hours of the day, in order to avoid dehydration. In their haste to find a cooler region, they loosen and stir up the earth. This activity allows oxygen, nitrogen, and other air- and waterborne elements to penetrate the garden's root systems, and at the same time it creates tunnels in the soil to facilitate root growth.

Aeration also stimulates the reproduction of invisible organisms, which feed on organic material and minerals trapped in the soil, releasing nitrogen, potassium, phosphorus, and humic acid, all of which are essential for green, healthy plants.

Oligochaetes are naturally obliged to swallow large quantities of soil as they burrow. However, they are equipped with an astonishingly muscular gullet and can easily digest any nutritive matter contained in the soil. Do not be deceived by appearances, though: oligochaetes are fastidious creatures. Rather than pollute their burrows, they tunnel upward after dark to deposit their waste products on the surface of the soil. These waste products, commonly referred to as castings, contain nitrogen, calcium, magnesium, phosphorus, and potassium. The digestive habits of a robust herd of oligochaetes can usually save the average gardener the trouble and expense of applying chemical fertilizer.

Bear in mind that oligochaetes will not live in any old pile of dirt. You will have to attract them by mixing organic fertilizers and manures in your garden soil and by surrounding your plants with a $\frac{1}{2}$-inch covering of organic mulch, which helps to keep the ground cool and moist. Avoid excessive tilling of the garden bed, since oligochaetes are not amused by having their homes destroyed and their bodies mutilated; rather, once you have dug your garden beds in spring, you are better off using a hoe or a thick covering of mulch to rid your bed of weeds. Finally, refrain as much as possible from using chemical fertilizers and pesticides, as these will corrode the digestive tract of oligochaetes beyond all repair.

While it is a peculiar trait of humankind to abhor that which does not fit its rather limited ideas of physical beauty, oligochaetes do not merit the disrespect traditionally heaped upon them. Rather than bruise their heads with our heels, we should offer thanks. For when treated with courtesy and common sense, these noble creatures never fail to repay us.

COMPOST

by Roger B. Swain

The subject hints of alchemy. Raw materials consisting of common wastes are transformed into something so sought after that there is never enough. Although the metamorphosis is dramatic, there is no great secret to how compost is made. Nor is there any one correct way to do it, despite the impression that may have been given by the volumes of information on the subject. At the risk of adding to the aura of mystery and exactitude surrounding compost, I here add my advice to the heap.

Compost is nothing more than partially decomposed organic matter, made up primarily of the remains of leaves, stems, and other plant parts. It is a dark, crumbly, pleasant-smelling substance that resembles what you would find were you to roll back a decaying log in the forest. Soil to which compost has been added can be worked more easily, holds more air, and water, and is less likely to erode. The compost provides some nutrients directly, and others indirectly by increasing their availability. All in all, those who see compost as a kind of vegetable gold are not far from the mark.

Unfortunately, although you start with a large volume of raw material when you make compost, you invariably end up with a small amount of concentrated end product. No matter how much there is of this, it never seems to stretch far enough. Somewhere between planting the rhubarb and top-dressing the hedge, you run out. When you have run out you can't just go out and buy more, although peat humus and composted cow manure will do in a pinch. No, you have to make it.

Most gardeners are in a hurry, and their impatience has led to the invention of numerous recipes for what I call fast compost. Fast compost takes advantage of human labor and attention to ensure an optimum environment for the growth of microbes and hence rapid decomposition. How soon the compost is ready for use depends on 1) moisture, 2) temperature, 3) aeration, 4) the surface area of the organic matter, and 5) a nitrogen supply. In the best of conditions, finished compost can be made in two weeks, though two months is a more reasonable goal.

The ingredients for quick compost must be assembled all at one time. Basically they are equal volumes of a carbon source (such as dry leaves, hay, straw, or seaweed) and a nitrogen source (such as grass clippings, weeds, or manure). More-concentrated nitrogen sources can also be used, ranging from ammonium sulfate to alfalfa meal, cottonseed meal, or blood meal, but lesser amounts of these are needed. Some recipes further recommend adding one part soil to the compost to inoculate the organic matter with organisms. All the ingredients should preferably be finely cut up. This can be done by hand with a machete and a chopping block or by machine. Either mix all the ingredients beforehand, or build the pile in thin alternating layers, each only a couple of inches deep. As the pile is built, hose it down so that the contents are thoroughly moistened. The minimum size for a completed pile is 4 feet in diameter and 4 feet high. So constructed, a pile should begin decomposing almost immediately. Rapid decomposition will generate heat, the pile reaching an internal temperature as high as 160°. This is hot enough to kill weed seeds and disease organisms inside the pile.

It is necessary to turn a fast compost pile now and then to keep the interior well aerated and to be sure the contents are uniformly moist. Turning also allows you to shift the undecayed matter on the outside of the pile into the interior. The easiest way to do this is to simply repile the compost heap adjacent to the old. The more frequently the pile is turned (once a week is not too often), the faster the material will decay. If the pile fails to heat up, you need to add more nitrogen. Finally, when the pile is no longer generating heat, the compost is ready for use. The faster the compost, the coarser the finished product is likely to be, but it is perfectly reasonable to spread it in the garden and let it finish breaking down there.

I confess I have never made fast compost, at least not intentionally. But I am an expert at making slow compost. I like slow compost because it takes so much less labor than fast compost. I don't have to assemble all the ingredients at once. Indeed, I can dispense with many of them altogether. The finished product may not be quite as rich, but in terms of nutrients gained for energy expended it is probably richer. As a way of recycling materials, slow compost cannot be beat, regardless of the time it takes.

Every fall, huge quantities of leaves drop from the trees in this town. Overwhelmed by their abundance, the neighbors work hard to get rid of them. In the past this meant burning; today it means loading them into bags and putting these out on the curb. Not only is this a waste of plastic bags, but it is also compost lost. And the people who assiduously dispose of their leaves each fall are the same ones who buy great big bags filled with peat moss each spring. Dead leaves, and nothing more, make a perfectly good substitute for peat moss if they are turned into leaf mold first. And the way to do that is with slow compost. You pile the leaves up, keep them moist, and wait.

Because loose leaves tend to blow over into the neighbor's yard, I corral mine inside circular bins made from wooden snow fencing. (A 50-foot section cut into three lengths will make three bins, each slightly more than 5 feet in diameter and 4 feet high.) It is surprising how many leaves one can put into a small volume. The leaves from this ⅓-acre yard neatly fit into a single one.

There is not enough nitrogen in dried leaves for decomposition to be rapid, but there are enough microbes present for it to get under way without the addition of soil or other activators. The pile should be concave at the top to funnel rainwater into the interior. The aim is to keep the leaves moist enough that a drop or two of water will appear when a sample of leaves from the interior of the pile is squeezed hard. By spring, I find that the pile has shrunk to half its height. I turn the pile once or twice during the summer, which breaks up the clumps of leaves, mixes in air, and speeds the breakdown. A year after the pile is made (or two if I have neglected my turning), my slow compost is ready.

There is, of course, nothing wrong with adding grass clippings, weeds, or vegetable kitchen wastes to a slow compost pile. When I have any organic matter to dispose of, I toss it on the heap. This gets mixed in when the pile is turned.

Finished slow compost is a dark, crumbly substance. I use mine without screening it, but it can be rubbed through a sieve made from 3/4-inch hardware cloth. Any pieces that are undecayed simply get tossed into the next compost pile.

There is never any danger of applying too much compost to a garden. If you have enough, add a 1-inch to 2-inch deep layer to the entire garden every year. In the case of a new garden, spread the compost and mix it into the top few inches of soil. Or else work a shovelful into the soil under each transplant as you put them in.

Whatever you do, do something with your compost. By definition, compost is only partially decayed and the metabolic fires continue to smolder, ultimately resulting in carbon dioxide and ash. Many a miser has tried to hang onto compost only to discover that the pile of black gold grows steadily smaller. Compost really only pays off when it has been generously spent.

Gardening Tools

by A. Wayne Cahilly

Tools, tools, tools! Where in the garden would I be without my tools? Every spring I watch the frantic hordes descend on the garden center near my home to replace all of their tools that failed. I can't participate; my tools didn't break, they performed superbly!

Understanding what you need is the first step to a successful relationship with your gardening tools. First, answer these questions about each of your gardening tasks: How often will the task be performed? What is the proper tool for the job? Can several of these tasks be accomplished with a single tool?

Once you have analyzed your needs, head to the garden center to "window shop." Pick up each tool and examine it. Is it repairable, light enough to use but strong enough to last? Is it the right tool for your particular job? Then, put the tools back and leave. Reassess your needs. Next Saturday is soon enough to part with your money.

Here are my five "must-have" tools for yard and garden upkeep:

1. **Spade.** I prefer a flat-bladed, square-tipped, D-handle spade with the back filled in where the handle and the blade meet. Mine is made by Ames and has been in use for 14 years. It's just getting broken in.

2. **Pruning shears.** I spare no expense here. Felco #2 shears fit my hand and are the best value I have found. Everything on them can be taken off and sharpened, cleaned, or lubricated. Other Felco models are equally well made, and best of all, all the parts can be replaced.

3. **Trowel.** This is what everyone was replacing at the garden center! Mine is made by Wilkinson Sword, and the blade and the shaft into the handle are one piece. Avoid trowels with tin handles or blades formed from "stamped" metal. Spare no expense. Buy one that has a forged, polished blade; has a comfortable handle; and measures no more than 12 inches tip to tip.

4. **Pruning saw.** Again it's Felco to the rescue; however, several other companies make very fine saws. Look for one that has an ARS-type blade. I like a narrow blade for working in shrubs and for light pruning. The blade should be stiff so it does not bend easily, and the handle should fit your hands. Be sure the locking mechanism on a folding saw locks securely.

5. **Rake.** Since I have limited space in which to store long-handled tools, I chose a modular type with one handle and several snap-in heads. I can attach a garden-rake head for leveling soil, or replace it with a fan-rake head for raking leaves in the fall. Several manufacturers have made this style; mine came from Burpee.

Regardless of what tool you select, care is essential if you want it to last. Clean digging tools with a rag to remove all soil, and coat them lightly with oil to prevent rust. Cutting tools should be cleaned with steel wool, oiled, and stored away from moisture. Sharpen your saw, shears, and spade when needed. A sharp tool works better and so will you.

Next spring you can smile as your neighbors and friends rush to the garden center to replace heavy, dull, rusty, broken gardening tools. After all, yours will be well selected, correctly cared for, properly stored, and waiting patiently for the gardening season to begin.

ON GATES AND PATHS
by Page Dickey

I have had a gate built for the beginning of the woodland path, and, weather permitting, it is to be installed this week. It will open a way through the barrier of deer fencing around the garden to a path that weaves through my sliver of woodland, returning, by way of the barn-yard, to the house.

How pleasant it will be to open that gate to the curving path as I go each day this spring to see the snowdrops and aconites and clumps of daffodils. There is something delicious in the ceremony of unlatching a gate that allows you to go on an adventure down a path, or to enter a hidden garden. It is a simple thing, a gate, but its presence adds an appealing mystery, an allurement to one's bit of land.

Just as a garden gate suggests the thrill of discovery, so can a garden path prolong the enjoyable suspense; it is what draws you in, what piques your curiosity. A path is especially enticing if it disappears from view around a bend or a flower bed, urging you to follow it to its destination. Even the smallest property can be made magical by gates and paths, just for the pleasure of walking—through gardens, under arbors, around the perimeter of the yard. Shrubs and trees can be planted to mask your way, giving a sense of privacy and surprise to that walk; and, by concealing one part of the yard from another, an otherwise dull piece of property becomes diverse and mysterious, and the path leading through its various parts an engaging entertainment.

The surface of a path can change as you progress along its way, from grass in the more formal areas, or any sort of combination of brick, stone, and gravel, to steppingstones in a rustic setting, or, as on my woodland trail, merely dirt lined with logs, marking a way 6 feet wide so that two people can walk comfortably side by side.

A neighbor asked me recently what, if anything, he should do to a wooded hillside that he looks onto across an old ice pond below his farmhouse. It is a handsome wood, partly a grove of mature beech trees, giving a silvery aura to its depth, and partly an old stand of white pines. Thinking how nice it would be not just to look upon this wood but to be drawn into it, to enjoy it in a more intimate way, I suggested a path to my friend.

Why not create a path for walking through his wood? A gate from his fenced garden already leads down a dirt road to a bridge over the stream into which his pond spills. From here a path could be cut up through the hillside of pines and into the beech grove, leading you from the dark shade of evergreens to the pale light among silver-barked beech trees, and then out to sunshine and water as you circle around the pond and back to the farmhouse. The idea delighted him, and immediately plans were made to stake it out.

The sight of a gate and a path through one's property excites the imagination, luring you from one area to another as a series of visual surprises unfold—from brook to beechwood, from meadow to pond, from white garden to woodland to barnyard. What a simple and satisfying way to transform your property and enhance your everyday garden pleasures.

VII FRIENDS

*"Nature never breaks
her own laws."*

Leonardo da Vinci

AND FOES

A
Loyal Friend,
a Link to Paradise

by Anne Raver

I was in Maryland two weeks ago, pruning the mock orange bushes. It was early morning, and I was the first one up. I had that delicious feeling of being able to listen to the birds and watch the mist rise off the fields without another consciousness, even a beloved one, commenting on the experience.

I missed my dog, Molly, with that kind of pain that doesn't really ever go away when you have loved someone. She was my companion for 14 years, and last fall I had to make that decision I'd been dreading for a couple of years, as I watched her begin to limp on our walks through the meadow, or falter and almost fall as we climbed the stairs to bed, and lose control of her bladder—a humiliating part of growing old for anyone—which made her blink and furrow her brow with shame.

"It's all right, Molly," we told her. "We love you. You're a good dog."

As the summer deepened, she no longer trotted behind me as I trundled my wheelbarrow to the compost pile. She didn't even watch from her favorite spot, a cool hole beneath the shade of the mock oranges that border the garden. She stayed mostly in the shadows of the cellar, lying against the cool stone wall.

The farm had become Molly's second home a few years ago, when I moved to New York City. I couldn't see her—or her cat friend, Mrs. Grey—twiddling their paws in an apartment. And after my father's death, my mother almost welcomed the company. They almost liked her *too* much, hardly blinking when my friends and I would get back in my old red Trooper and head for the city.

One afternoon in November, my mother called me at work. Molly had stopped eating and drinking, so she had taken her to our veterinarian,

Dr. Earle Flick, who was keeping her at the hospital for some tests. She was severely anemic, so he hooked her up to an IV. Then he found a tumor in her spleen. If he operated, and the cancer hadn't spread, she might have six months to a year—though that wouldn't solve her other problems, like failing legs and incontinence.

I went down to the farm the next day to be with my friend and to think things over. I knew my mother couldn't be constantly cleaning up after Molly, or lifting her in and out of the house. And even if she had six months more, what kind of life would it be?

But thinking about putting her to sleep—that euphemism we use because it's hard to say "I killed her"—was like facing some great black wall. To take a life assumes terrible power. It feels like a sin, a transgression against nature, even if you tell yourself it will stop the suffering. And it brings you up against the incomprehensibility of the spirit. Who was I to extinguish the light that made Molly *Molly*—and no one else?

It was Indian summer that day in November when I pulled into the farm. The soybean fields had turned a coppery gold and the air smelled of toasted leaves. I called Dr. Flick, who said that Molly had perked up on the IV. So I said I'd like to take her home for the day, to take a walk over the fields—and say goodbye.

I'd gotten Molly as a puppy when I was married and lived on a salt marsh in Ipswich, Massachusetts. She grew up eating clamshells and chasing rabbits and seagulls. She learned to swim in the river and the bay, because she couldn't bear losing sight of us. We were her pack.

Molly was a shepherd-collie mix, with a big white ruff and a fluffy white tail that sailed out behind her when she ran. But deep in her soul, she was also that first wolf, tamed by some cave family 15,000 years ago.

When we let our marriage unravel, I kept Molly. We hadn't planned it that way. It just happened: that ineffable connection between two souls, be they human or animal.

I have always felt it is human arrogance that assumes that only people have souls. In *The Unbearable Lightness of Being*, Milan Kundera points out that Genesis, which gives man dominion over the animals, "was written by a man, not a horse." He goes on to say that man probably invented God "to sanctify the dominion that he had usurped for himself over the cow and the horse."

Amen. I love this book, which is a study of

love, because it has three main characters: a man and a woman and a dog. And when the two lovers, Tomas and Tereza, are watching their dog, Karenin, die of cancer, Tereza has a sacrilegious thought: that she loves Karenin more than she does Tomas. Because the love between dog and human is so unconditional—and so completely selfless.

You don't try to make a dog over in your own image. You don't say, "If she would be wittier at dinner parties, I could love her." You don't wonder, "Do I love her more than she loves me?"

Dogs, Mr. Kundera says, are our link to Paradise. They don't know evil or jealousy or discontent. To sit with a dog on a hillside on a glorious afternoon is to be back in Eden, where doing nothing was not boring—it was peace.

My brother's family had come down to the farm, too, that golden day—now distilled in my mind like some last day in Paradise—and his little girls and I took Molly for her favorite walk. We followed the path we always had: down the lane past the barn, over the hills bordered by black walnuts, to the stream where the deer bed down. We sat for a long time, listening to the sound of water. We listened to the birds and insects and felt the sun on our backs.

Then I took her back to the hospital, and asked Dr. Flick to give her an injection. I held my arms around her as he stroked her head and told her he loved her and put the needle in her vein.

I wasn't prepared for how quick her death was. I'd expected, somehow, to have a minute or two left. To say one more goodbye, I guess. To apologize for taking her life.

But she slumped to the floor as if whatever force we call life—some call it breath—had been let out of her in an instant. And she was gone. All that animal joy. The pleasure she took in the here and now. A bone, the wind in her face, being next to me.

We wrapped her in an old embroidered tablecloth, steeped in the memories of happy meals in our sunlit kitchen. And we buried her on the crest of a hill that looks south over the rolling fields. My brother and I dug the hole and laid her in it. We picked the last of the summer's roses and placed them on her head. My mother helped shovel in the honest dirt.

Tears streamed down our faces as we buried our friend. And our voices cracked as we sang a few hymns on that golden afternoon. Then we went up to the house and broke out our finest Scotch, and talked about Molly, and the other great dogs we had known.

I may have another dog someday, but never one like Molly. She was my kindred spirit. And I was lucky to know her.

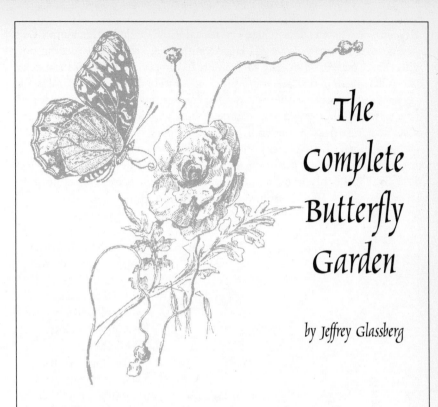

The Complete Butterfly Garden

by Jeffrey Glassberg

What gardener can resist butterflies and the beauty, drama and movement they bring to the garden? No matter how small your garden, you will be able to grow some plants that invite butterflies into your yard. A single butterfly bush will attract many of the butterflies already present in your area; a few parsley plants might well entice an elegant black swallowtail. But done correctly, butterfly gardening can actually create new populations of butterflies.

The key here is to create a real butterfly garden. When you make a garden, you usually grow plants. When you butterfly-garden, you should aspire to grow butterflies! How do you do this? By having food plants for both the caterpillars and the butterflies. Plants that feed both are absolutely necessary to foster a healthy population of butterflies.

Feeding the Caterpillars

Almost all butterfly caterpillars eat plants. As a gardener, your natural reflex may have been to kill (or at least remove) anything you found eating your plants. But unlike many moth caterpillars, butterfly caterpillars aren't real pests in the garden. Tiger Swallowtail caterpillars feeding on wild cherry leaves, or viceroy caterpillars feeding on willows, or monarch caterpillars feeding on a stand of milkweed—rarely do they cause any lasting harm. And because they eat only special groups of plants, you don't have to worry about them "spreading." They will definitely turn up their noses at your roses, rhododendrons and rosemary.

So try to positively enjoy the caterpillars you find on the plants-- they will soon become the butterflies you desire. Besides, on close inspection, you'll probably find that many of the caterpillars are fascinating and beautiful in their own right.

Feeding the Adults

Now that you have created new butterflies by providing caterpillar food plants, you'll certainly want to consider the care and well-being of the adults. Luckily, the number-one food for adult butterflies is nectar. With flowers as their nectar source, you have many options. And there's no law that says that the flowers can't be beautiful!

Encouraging Heterogeneity

Different butterflies use different caterpillar food plants; likewise different butterflies prefer different nectar sources. Some favor large flowers, many fancy small. Skippers seem to be especially drawn to purple flowers, while many Hairstreaks like white flowers. Others feed on small, inconspicuous plants that most gardeners would regard as weeds. (Try planting these in a hidden corner.)

The more complex your garden becomes, the more attractive it is likely to be to butterflies. Do remember, the closer your garden is to an existing population of butterflies, the more likely it is that they will find and use the special plants in your garden.

So go ahead—indulge your passions for gardening and for these splendid creatures. As you create new populations of butterflies, your passions will have beneficial applications for us all.

Other good *nectar* sources include:

- Butterfly bush (*Buddleia davidii;* when this bush blooms, it is usually the most attractive plant for butterflies).
- Globe amaranth (*Gomphrena globosa*)
- Heliotrope (*Heliotropium arborescens*)
- Lavender (*Lavandula angustifolia*)
- Lilies, Oriental hybrids (*Lilium rubrum*, aromatic cultivars; these drive Tiger Swallowtails wild!).
- Marigold (*Tagetes)*
- Privet (*Ligustrum japonicum*)
- Stonecrop (*Sedum spectabile*)
- Thyme (*Thymus)*
- Zinnia (*Zinnia elegans*, the single-flowered varieties are much more attractive to butterflies).

This Type of plant . . .	Attracts this type of butterfly . . .	Found in this region of the U.S. . . .
Asters	Pearl Crescent; Field Crescent	Entire U.S.
Buckwheats	Acmon Blue; Blue Copper; Mormon Metalmark; and others	Western U.S. only
Cassia spp.	Little Yellow; Sleepy Orange; Cloudless Sulphur	Mainly the South
Ceanothus	Mottled Duskywing and Pacuvius Duskywing	East and West, respectively.
Citrus	Giant Swallowtail	Southeast
Columbine	Columbine Duskywing	Northeast
Dutchman's pipe (*Aristolochia durior*)	Pipevine Swallowtail	Eastern and southwestern California
Hackberry	Hackberry Emperor; Tawny Emperor, American Snout; Question Mark	Eastern two-thirds of the U.S.
Lupines	Melissa Blue and other blues	Mainly in the West
Mallows/hollycocks	Gray Hairstreak; West Coast Lady; Common Checkered-Skipper	
Milkweeds (*Asclepias*)	Monarch	Entire U.S.
Parsley	Black Swallowtail; Anise Swallowtail	Entire U.S.
Passion-vine	Gulf Fritillary	Southern half of the U.S.

This Type of plant . . .	Attracts this type of butterfly . . .	Found in this region of the U.S. . . .
Pearly everlastings (*Gnaphalium*)	American Lady	Entire U.S.
Rock cresses (*Arabis*)	Orangetips; Marbles	Entire U.S.
Purpletop grass	Common Wood-Nymph; Little Glassywing; Zabulon Skipper	Most of the U.S.
Sassafras (small tree)	Spicebush Swallowtail	East
Snapdragon (*Antirrhinum majurs*)	Common Buckeye	Most of the U.S.
Sunflower (*Heliantbus annuus*)	Gorgone Checkerspot	Central U.S.
Turtlehead (*Chelone glabra*)	Baltimore Checkerspot	East
Violets	Greater and Lesser Fritillaries	Entire U.S.
Wild cherries	Tiger Swallowtails; Coral Hairstreak; Spring Azure	Entire U.S.
Wild indigo	Wild Indigo Duskywing	East
Willows	Mourning Cloak; Viceroy; Red-spotted Purple; Lorquin's Admiral; Weidenmeyer's Admiral; Acadoam and Sylvan Hairstreaks	Entire U.S.

Bees Do It

by Eric Swanson

I'd been waiting near the garden for almost half an hour before my informant arrived.

"Pleazze ztay quite ztill," came a soft voice at my right ear. "Zudden movementz ztartle me, and I might zting you." My informant sighed. "Then, az I attempted to pull my zting from your body, part of my abdomen would rip away, and that would be ze end of me. Only Her Royal Majezzty (may she live a thouzzand dayz!) can zurvive ze zting."

Naturally, I agreed to keep movement to a minimum. "Er," I added, "if you don't mind my asking, are you male or female?"

"Zuch crude dizztinctionz! How typical of your zpeciez! I am a Worker, which I zuppoze would correzpond to ze ordinary female of your zoziety, although Her Royal Majezzty (may she live a thouzzand dayz!) iz ze only female capable of breeding. The malez of our zpeciez are called Dronez. Zey're only good for fertilizing Her Royal Majezzty. A few zecondz of pleazure and zey die."

"What does a Worker do?"

A contented humming filled my ear—by which I surmised, nervously, that my informant had settled inside it. "We gather pollen and nectar to feed ze colony," she whispered. "We build and clean ze hive. We warm it with our bodiez and cool it with our wingz."

"Yes, about pollen and nectar . . . " I ventured.

"Pollen zuppliez protein for our babiez. We go from flower to flower, gathering pollen on our hind legz, and afterward depozit it directly inzide ze zellz where each child is raized. We alzo drink nectar from each flower we vizit, and convert it into honey in zpecial zacz in our ezophagi. When we return to ze hive, we reguritate ze honey into honeycombzz, where it thickenzz. Honey (may it flow a thouzzand dayz!) iz ze prinzipal food of adult beez."

"Don't you lose some of the pollen you gather?" I asked.

"We do not loze anything! We give! We vizit only a zingle zpeciez of plant in ze courze of every trip outzide ze hive. Onze we locate a zourze of food, we gather pollen from ze male organ of each blozzom and depozit a few crumbz onto ze female organ. Many zpezies can only produze offzpring becauze we vizit zem, or produze far more abundantly with our azziztance zan without it. Zeze would include most of ze fruitz and vegetablez zo dear to humanzz. It iz true zat many blozzomz are capable of pollinating themzelvez, but our work zervez to produce zeedz of better quality, which enzurez zat each new generation of a given zpeciez will be healthy and ztrong. Zat iz ze Great Danze."

"We call it cross-pollination."

"Zzzz! An ugly phraze!"

"Yes, I'm afraid we humans are awfully unromantic. Tell me, though, since it's clear that bees play such an important role, what can we do to make sure you'll visit our gardens?"

My informant brushed seductively against my earlobe. "Zuch a zweet queztion! We love fruit treez, of courze. But on a zmaller zcale, you could plant azters and zweet clover, which make lovely borderz. We are alzo very fond of catnip, borage, zunflowerz, Queen Anne'z laze, and goldenrod. Ze zmell of zeze iz quite attractive to our kind. Az a lazt rezort, you could even purchaze a colony from a beekeeper. We are quite tranzportable and adapt to many different zituationz. You might even try building a lovely box for uz out of wood and plazing it near your garden. We might make our home inzide it, but zen again we might not."

"Is there anything we should avoid? Anything you don't like?"

My informant shuddered. "Pezztizidezz!" she hissed.

And suddenly, as if to prove her point, she was gone.

The Trouble with Deer

by Charlotte M. Frieze

In all climate zones deer have gone from being a beloved wild species to backyard enemy number one. Gardeners feel utterly defenseless as these green gangsters waltz across the lawn to dine on a bountiful harvest of vegetables, shrubs, and perennials. Where homeowners once erected ornamental deer statues, they now install electric fencing. But for those who prefer détente to nuclear warfare, careful plant selection can be a good way to protect your garden from these hungry beasts.

As with most creatures, including humans, a deer's appetite is directly influenced by his sense of smell. Deer generally prefer a bland diet and will avoid strong, pungent plants. Show a deer a row of perfect pink tea roses and his appetite alarm will sound, but offer him a row of lemon balm and sage and he'll trot on by. And remember, deer are real sissies. Just spread a little coyote urine, blood meal, or other deer repellents around the garden and their instincts will steer them clear.

It's the chef who prepares the spiciest garden who has the fewest furry diners. Whip up a menu of plants with the aroma of mint, lemon, or sage and you're apt to find the deer lining up for your neighbor's deliciously tempting and colorful bed of daylilies or hostas. But remember, a starving deer will nibble at anything! So if your garden is a McDonald's along a popular deer highway, your best option will be a combination of aromatic plants and wire or net deer fencing 8 to 10 feet high.

When planning your garden, place deer-resistant plants in front of the most appetizing ones to discourage deer from stomping deeper into the beds. In addition to most herbs, the following plants should discourage the casual browser.

ANNUALS
Ageratum houstonianum (Ageratum)
Ipomoea purpurea (Morning glory)
Matthiola incana (Stock)
Salvia splendens (Salvia)
Tagetes spp. (Marigold)
Tithonia rotundifolia (Mexican sunflower)
Tropaeolum majus (Nasturtium)

PERENNIALS
Achillea var. (Yarrow)
Asclepias tuberosa (Butterfly weed)
Aster novae-angliae (New England aster)
Astilbe × *arendsii* (Astilbe)
Coreopsis verticillata (Threadleaf coreopsis)
Echinacea purpurea (Purple coneflower)
Iris spp. (Iris)
Monarda didyma (Bee balm)
Perovskia hybrids (Russian sage)
Rudbeckia spp. (Black-eyed Susan)
Salvia spp. (Perennial salvia)

BULBS
Allium spp. (Flowering onion)
Crocus spp. (Crocus)
Muscari armeniacum (Grape hyacinth)
Narcissus spp. (Daffodil, narcissus)
Scilla siberica (Siberian squill)

GROUND COVERS
Ajuga reptans (Bugleweed)
Arctostaphylos uva-ursi (Bearberry)
Cerastium tomentosum (Snow-in-summer)
Convallaria majalis (Lily-of-the-valley)
Cotoneaster spp. (Cotoneaster)
Galium odoratum (Sweet woodruff)
Juniperus spp. (Juniper)
Lamium maculatum (Dead nettle)
Pachysandra terminalis (Japanese pachysandra)
Sedum spp. (Sedum)

VINES
Clematis spp. (Clematis)
Euonymus fortunei var. *radicans* (Wintercreeper)
Hedera helix (English ivy)
Lonicera spp. (Honeysuckle)
Parthenocissus quinquefolia (Virginia creeper)
Parthenocissus tricuspidata (Boston ivy)
Polygonum aubertii (Silver lace vine)
Wisteria spp. (Wisteria)

SHRUBS
Berberis var. (Barberry)
Buxus var. (Boxwood)
Forsythia var. (Forsythia)
Hibiscus syriacus (Rose-of-Sharon)
Ilex opaca (American holly)
Magnolia var. (Magnolia)
Pieris japonica var. (Japanese andromeda)
Pinus mugo (Mugo pine)
Spiraea var. (Bridal wreath)
Syringa vulgaris (Lilac)

BIENNIALS
Digitalis purpurea (Foxglove)
Myosotis var. (Forget-me-nots)

Additional Plants for the South

PERENNIALS
Agave spp.
Aloe spp.
Erigeron karvinskianus (Mexican daisy)
Gerbera jamesonii (Gerbera daisy)
Geum quellyon (Geum)
Osteospermum fruticosum (Freeway daisy)

BULBS
Allium sphaerocephalum (Ornamental garlic)
Hymenocallis narcissiflora (Peruvian daffodil)

GROUND COVERS
Gazania (Gazania)
Lantana spp. (Lantana)
Vinca major (Big leaf periwinkle)

VINES
Bougainvillea (Bougainvillea)
Gelsemium sempervirens (Carolina jessamine)

SHRUBS
Cassia spp. (Cassia)
Cupressus spp. (Cypress)
Cycas spp. (Cycad)
Leucothoe axillaris (Coastal leucothoe)
Mahonia bealei (Leatherleaf mahonia)
Myrtus communis (True myrtle)
Nandina domestica (Nandina)
Nerium oleander (Oleander)
Pittosporum spp. (Pittosporum)
Rosmarinus officinalis (Rosemary)

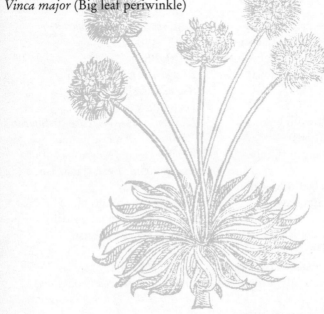

America's Least Wanted:
The Dirty Dozen

by Stephanie Flack

Illustrations by Megan Grey Rollins

This is a rogues' gallery unlike all others. No human villains stare menacingly from these pages. The lineup contains 12 invasive plants and animals—all introduced by human activities into areas outside their native range. Scientists call these species "invasive exotics." They also call them problems.

In their natural habitats, these species are held in check by the powerful forces of competition, predation, or disease. Unleashed in new environments, however, they can wreak havoc on indigenous species and ecological communities.

Some of these alien species were originally introduced into their new homes on purpose, to solve a problem or even just to provide a pretty sight. Others made their way by accident, like the stowaway zebra mussel and brown tree snake.

These transplanted miscreants are ruthless in their quest for light, water, space, nutrients, or the very flesh of their victims. Sometimes they also transform the natural areas that they invade—changing soil composition, making lands more prone to catastrophic fire, or, like the insidious tamarisk tree, sucking up scarce water in the arid Southwest.

Not all exotic species are bad, though. Some, like soybeans and wheat, contribute greatly to our economy. Of the roughly 4,000 exotic plants and 2,300 exotic animals in the United States, only about 15 percent are considered "harmful" according to a 1993 U.S. Office of Technology Assessment report. However, this small percentage can have a big impact: from 1906 to 1991, a scant 79 exotic species exacted about $97 billion in damages.

Prevention is the best solution. Once exotic species gain a toehold in natural communities, controlling them can demand huge outlays of time, money, and effort. As The Nature Conservancy's wildland weeds specialist John Randall explains, "Our best bet is to keep these troublemakers out, or to be vigilant in finding them early, before they can set up shop in our natural areas and ecosystems." Meet the "Dirty Dozen"—and learn what you can do to help prevent their spread.

ZEBRA MUSSEL (*Dreissena polymorpha*)—This thumbnail-size mollusk can shut down electrical utilities by clogging water intake pipes and can cause millions of dollars in damages every year. The mussel has spread throughout the waterways of the Great Lakes and the Mississippi River Basin.

FLATHEAD CATFISH (*Pylodictus olivarus*)—Native to the lower Great Lakes, the Mississippi River Basin, and parts of the Gulf Slope drainage, the flathead catfish was introduced into the Colorado River and North Carolina's Cape Fear River as well as other parts of the country as a sportfish. But unlike other catfish, the flathead is not a scavenger but a voracious predator; it gobbles up native fishes in the rivers where it has been introduced.

LEAFY SPURGE (*Euphorbia esula*)—Both ranchers and conservationists would love to rid their lands of leafy spurge. This prolific plant was first recorded in the United States in 1827, when it was introduced either by accident (in a mix of agricultural seed) or intentionally (because of its attractive yellow flowers). This weed infests more than 3 million acres in the United States and reduces the productivity of grazing land by 50 to 75 percent because cattle cannot eat it.

TAMARISK (*Tamarix* species)—In the arid Southwest, water is precious and the tamarisk is a serious threat to this resource. The tree sucks 5 million acre-feet of water a year and its roots are able to reach water tables below the desert floor. It was introduced in the 1800s by settlers as a source of shade, erosion control, and wood but now infests about 1 million acres in the United States.

ROSY WOLFSNAIL (*Euglandina rosea*)—First introduced into the Hawaiian Islands as a way of controlling the African tree snail, the rosy wolfsnail soon became the enemy of the islands' abundant endemic snails. Also locally known as the "cannibal snail," the rosy wolfsnail is a hungry predator that has eaten so many of Hawaii's native snails that some are now extinct.

GREEN CRAB (*Carcinus maenas*)—A recent accidental introduction to the San Francisco Bay, the European green crab has spread quickly because of its voracious and indiscriminating appetite. If allowed to spread, the green crab could alter natural food webs and damage West Coast oyster and Dungeness crab fisheries.

HYDRILLA (*Hydrilla verticillata*)—Like its namesake the mythological Hydra, this plant seems nearly impossible to kill. Since being introduced into Florida waters for cultivation for aquariums, this weed has managed to infest nearly half of the state's public waterways. Hydrilla can grow as much as 10 inches in a day and clogs waterways so thoroughly that they are inaccessible to boaters and swimmers.

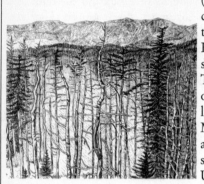

BALSAM WOOLY ADELGID (*Adelges piceae*)—Bad things also can come in small packages. This diminutive aphidlike insect has killed acres of Fraser firs in western North Carolina, southern Virginia, and eastern Tennessee by sucking out the firs' sap over several years. It has killed virtually all the adult firs in Great Smoky Mountains National Park, eliminating almost three-quarters of all the spruce-fir forest in the southern United States.

MICONIA (*Miconia calvescens*)—The Tahitians call this native of Latin America the "green cancer." The plant, which was introduced into Tahiti through three ornamental plantings in 1937, now covers nearly 70 percent of the island's forests. Hawaii could be next. It has already been found in 36 locations covering 11,000 acres on Maui, Oahu, Kauai, and the Big Island of Hawaii. Miconia can grow to nearly 50 feet tall, and its giant leaves block sun required for other vegetation to survive.

CHINESE TALLOW (*Sapium sebiferum*)—This tree was originally brought to South Carolina in the 1700s, but in the early 1900s the U.S. Department of Agriculture promoted tallow plantings in the Gulf Coast to start a local soap industry from the oil in its seeds. The tree flourishes wherever it is planted, and its leaves produce toxins that alter soil chemistry, making it impossible for native vegetation to grow.

PURPLE LOOSESTRIFE (*Lythrum salicaria*)—This deadly beauty is graced with bright purple flowers and has spread throughout the United States. It was originally introduced as an ornamental plant but is now a serious threat to wetlands in the Northeast and the Upper Midwest.

BROWN TREE SNAKE (*Boiga irregularis*)—The final member of our rogues' gallery is not so much a plague as it is a threat. The nocturnal snake, native to the Solomon Islands, Papua New Guinea, and Australia, was accidentally introduced into Guam through military transports in the 1940s. Since then, it has eliminated virtually all the native birds on the island. It also scales power lines, causing power outages once

every four days. More than 200 people have been treated for bites from these snakes in Guam. The bad news is that the brown tree snake has already been found in Hawaii six times, and experts say without major prevention improvements, it is only a matter of time before Hawaii—or even parts of the U.S. mainland—suffers the ravages of this predator.

What You Can Do to Help

1. Know your own backyard—learn to identify the most threatening pests in your area and how to report new invasions to appropriate authorities.
2. Landscape with native species or noninvasive ornamental plants.
3. Don't release pets or aquarium plants and fish into the environment.
4. Avoid disturbing natural areas—disturbance makes them more vulnerable to invasions by alien species.
5. Mail-order wisely and ask friends not to send you plants or animals through the mail.
6. Don't bring plants, fruits, soil, or animals into the country from abroad—or to Hawaii from the mainland—without having them inspected by quarantine officials; fill out agricultural declaration forms completely and honestly.

continued

7. Clean boats and other water equipment before transporting them from one body of water to another to avoid spreading aquatic pests such as zebra mussels or hydrilla. Leave behind unused bait and bucket water.

8. Clean your boots and camping gear before setting out for other regions or countries and again before returning home. When packing with horses, make sure that feed is certified weed-free.

9. Spread the word—educate yourself and others about the problem of alien species.

10. Get involved—join volunteer efforts to turn back aliens in natural areas such as your local conservancy preserves or state and national parks.

This article was adapted from "America's Least Wanted: Alien Species Invasions of U.S. Ecosystems," part of The Nature Conservancy's NatureServe program, sponsored by Canon U.S.A. The full report is available on the conservancy's website at http://www.tnc.org/science/library.

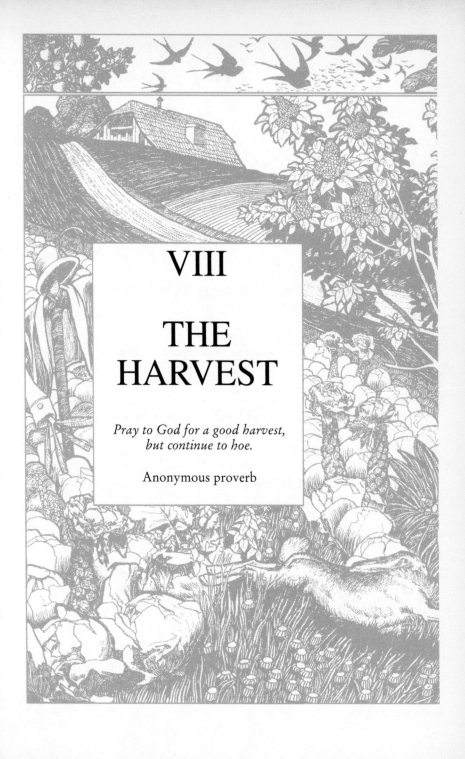

VIII

THE HARVEST

Pray to God for a good harvest,
but continue to hoe.

Anonymous proverb

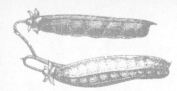

Harvest Lore

by Adele Q. Brown

As gardeners learn from their more knowledgeable mentors, a native wisdom continues to evolve that incorporates experience with belief. To explain the vagaries of nature or to foretell the harvest, a gentle lore unfolds.

Planting:
- The most fruitful time to plant is on the days ruled by Scorpio, Pisces, Taurus, or Cancer.
- Sow peas and beans in the wane of the moon; who soweth them sooner, soweth too soon.
- Sow fennel, sow trouble.
- Plant catnip and the cats will get it, sow it and the cats won't know it.
- Planting rue in your garden will deter Japanese beetles.

Foretelling the Harvest:
- Much snow, much hay.
- A mild winter and cold summer mean a poor harvest.
- If it rains on June 8, a wet harvest will follow.
- No sun, no showers, no summer flowers.
- When ladybugs arrive, expect a good crop.
- Early insects, early spring, good crops.

Corny Lore:
- A late spring is favorable to corn but not cattle.
- Thunder in March, corn to parch.
- Sow corn when oak leaves are the size of a mouse's ear.
- Corn planted in Leo will have small ears.
- In planting corn, four kernels to a hill: one for the blackbird, one for the crow, one for the cutworm, and one to grow.
- More corn grows in crooked rows.
- Corn should be knee-high by the Fourth of July.
- Don't shuck your corn till the cows come home.
- A full ear of corn will bend its head; an empty ear will stand upright.
- An armful of weeds is worth an ear of corn.

MINTOMANIA

by Marty Ross

Gardeners today often complain that mint is invasive, but, as I recall, my grandmother never gave it a chance to go far. Every evening, a large pitcher of iced tea, glistening with condensation, and with two or three big sprigs of mint jammed down among the ice cubes, stood its post at one corner of the dining-room table. There were a couple of mint leaves in every tall glass, and when our glasses were empty, we children liked to bruise the leaves with our long-handled spoons, swirl them around in the undissolved sugar at the bottom of the glasses, and drain the liquid in one delicious sip. Then, of course, we ate the ice.

Mint is a perennial herb; about 25 species and thousands of hybrids are known. Plants of the genus *Mentha* are characterized by square stems with leaves directly opposite each other along the stem. Some varieties grow up to 3 feet tall; others are low-growing ground covers. Mint leaves may be quilted or smooth and slightly hairy, rough, or glossy. To crush them between your fingers and inhale the sweet scent, or to nibble a leaf in the garden, is to take in the pure and undiluted essence of summer.

Mint thrives in sun and tolerates part shade, where it grows a bit leggy but is still vigorous. It is not bothered by pests or diseases. Mint loves moisture, but it must be planted in well-drained soil. In my family, cuttings of mint were always planted near an outside spigot, where they spread happily and required absolutely no care. The plants flower in late summer, at which time the essential oils in the leaves are at their peak. The flower spikes, which appear at the end of stems, like basil, are usually a soft purple. This is the time to harvest mint and dry the leaves for tea.

Some mint connoisseurs grow chocolate mint, spearmint and peppermint, Corsican mint, apple or pineapple mint, every kind of mint. Most gardeners grow good old traditional spearmint, and this is the flavor we recognize in mint juleps and other summer drinks. Peppermint is used in candy and medicines. Herb specialists and nurseries usually offer several varieties, but the best way to acquire mint is the old-fashioned way: ask a friend for a start.

Mint takes hold quickly from cuttings or divisions of small clumps dug up from the garden. You can even buy sprigs of mint at the grocery store and keep them in a glass of water until roots develop, or plant them directly in the garden. It does spread rapidly, but if you have a taste for mint, you'll be able to keep it under control. A few spearmint leaves frozen in ice cubes are delicious in a summer drink; chopped mint livens up a salad of sliced tomatoes. Mint freshens up summer bouquets, and it lasts a lot longer than most cut flowers, besides.

I've never kept mint in a pot on a windowsill in winter, and I doubt it would be happy, but while summer lasts, I think I'll put a little mint in everything.

Discovering the Scarlet Runner

Notes on synchronicity during a Maine Summer

by Paula Deitz

"Scarlet runner" is the common name for Phaseolus coccineus, *a perennial twining bean grown as an annual in cold countries and valued for its brilliant scarlet flowers and its pods with large, edible red-and-black seeds. It belongs to the pea family, and the blossoms are pollinated by hummingbirds,* Trochilidae, *who like other flower birds show a natural preference for red above other colors.*

Until last summer, when I read Nathaniel Hawthorne's novel *The House of the Seven Gables,* I knew little of the pleasures of observing the association between hummingbirds and red flowers. In general, I reserve my Maine summers for reading 19th-century English and American novels that amplify my enjoyment of rural life. I am especially drawn to Hawthorne's vivid depiction of the attitudes and customs of New England daily life that have permeated the region since Colonial days. In writing so intimately about characters of an earlier time, he made of the past another present. If you observe life today on the Maine coast, where change comes gradually, you are quite likely to encounter real people straight out of Hawthorne's novels.

The House of the Seven Gables is a perfect book for summer reading. The mysterious plot unfolds throughout one New England summer and climaxes in the brisk days of autumn. If you read slowly, as I do, you can pace yourself to finish the novel in early September, thus enriching your sense of the change in seasons and the weather.

One late afternoon in midsummer, reading on my screened porch overlooking the bay, I came across this luxuriant passage halfway through *Seven Gables*:

When the bean-vines began to flower on the poles, there was one particular variety which bore a vivid scarlet blossom. The Daguerreotypist had found these beans in a garret, over one of the seven gables, treasured up in an old chest of drawers, by some horticultural Pyncheon of days gone by, who, doubtless, meant to sow them the next summer, but was himself first sown in Death's garden-ground. By way of testing whether there was still a living germ in such ancient seeds, Holgrave had planted some of them; and the result of his experiment was a splendid row of bean-vines, clambering, early, to the full height of the poles, and arraying them, from top to bottom, in a spiral profusion of red blossoms. And, ever since the unfolding of the first bud, a multitude of humming-birds had been attracted thither. At times, it seemed as if for every one of the hundred blossoms there was one of these tiniest fowls of the air; a thumb's bigness of burnished plumage hovering and vibrating about the bean-poles. It was with indescribable interest, and even more than childish delight, that Clifford watched the humming-birds.

Often on summer mornings in Maine, I am gently awakened by the low vibrations of hummingbirds feeding on nectar from the honeysuckle vine outside my bedroom window. Watching these creatures is a delight that lingers in one's mind. But Hawthorne, bringing together the brilliant scarlet of the bean blossoms, the activity of the birds, and the "yellow richness" of late afternoon sun, created a new vision for my mind's eye. I had not yet actually seen a scarlet runner, but the image was as strong as if I had. As I read on in the novel, I realized too that this image functioned as an omen of the Pyncheon family's renewal and its emergence into an era of good fortune.

On August 2, I received a colorful letter from my friend Rosemary Porter, an English psychiatrist who now lives on a farm in upstate New York:

I hope your summer is progressing well. We have had some lovely sunny days picnicking and swimming at the pond. Our hay has been cut and our garden is burgeoning, particularly some pole beans with orange/red flowers that seem to be favorites of hummingbirds and monarch butterflies.

My immediate reaction was yes, I know, I have seen them in a garden of my own. I felt great pleasure in this new bond.

Later that month I forged a similar bond while visiting Harborside, Maine, a vegetable farming area on Cape Rosier. Harborside has become a center for organic farming, thanks to the famous self-sufficiency pioneers Scott and Helen Nearing, who, despite the handicaps of a cold climate and a short growing season, were the first to turn this rough coastal terrain into arable land. Their hearty spirit attracts disciples who settle new farms, some of which are planted in the manner of formal gardens.

Friends who live there invited me for an afternoon's visit. Following a late lunch, we decided to drop in on the Nearings, who receive between 3:30 and 5:30 P.M. Able-bodied guests are expected to lend a hand with whatever chores Scott happens to be doing, and Scott, now in his nineties, still does a hard day's work on a meticulous schedule.

Helen Nearing greeted us at the door of their stone farmhouse, and we stood in the yard and talked for a few minutes. The air was aglow in the slanting rays of late afternoon sun. She needed time to locate the field where Scott was working so that she could send us out to join him. "While you are waiting," she said, "why don't you walk down the path there a way, and you'll see the scarlet runner beans and the hummingbirds all over them."

In the fading light, the tiny blossoms were a deep scarlet, and in their hundreds adorned the tall poles from top to bottom. Everything around me was still except for the whirring of delicate hummingbirds darting from flower to flower. It occurred to me as I stood there that at some moment Nathaniel Hawthorne must have perceived the pure loveliness of what I witnessed, and that my life was now extending backward into his. What Hawthorne and I and Rosemary Porter all felt on observing the scarlet runner seemed to be a single experience.

Within a day or two I answered Rosemary Porter's letter, telling her this story and quoting the passage from *Seven Gables*. As an admirer of Jung and his theory of the synchronicity of events, she understood perfectly. I think that Hawthorne would have understood it, too.

Soon after Labor Day, I drove back to New York City. On the way, I stopped at Salem, Massachusetts, to see the actual House of the Seven Gables, now maintained as a permanent museum and tourist attraction. The house, where Hawthorne's cousin Susan Ingersoll once lived and which the writer loved to visit, fulfilled my expectations. The garden, at least as Hawthorne describes it, is not there, but it continues to flourish in his novel and in the minds and memories of his readers.

Not long after my return to New York, I received a small package in the mail. I unwrapped it and found a paper box of metallic red. Inside the box were a dozen of the largest, smoothest beans I had ever seen. They were deep purple-black tinged with pinkish red. With them was a brief note from Rosemary Porter:

Scarlet Runner Pole Beans

When the soil is warm and moderately dry, plant seed around rough poles, 3 ft. apart each way. Use 5 or 6 seeds per pole and thin to 3 plants. Cover seed 1" to 2" deep. Will grow over 6'.

Seed grown and fertilized by ruby-throated hummingbirds on Grasmere Farm, Callicoon, N.Y.

The best planting month is mid-May, or after the danger of frost is past. I hope you enjoy your scarlet flowers—and hummingbirds—as much as I have enjoyed mine.

Everlasting Flowers

by Daiva K. Gasperetti

One of the great pleasures of growing flowers is using the blossoms to enhance the rooms of our homes. Nothing adds spark to a dining table like a sumptuous centerpiece, while a nosegay in the powder room greets guests with a pleasant surprise. Yet fresh flowers last only a few days. Dried flowers, on the other hand, will last for months and sometimes years. Numerous varieties suitable for drying will readily grow in your own garden. But remember, harvesting flowers can render unattractive gaps, so plan your cutting garden in a separate area, much as you would a vegetable patch.

An amazingly brilliant palette of hues can be achieved with dried flowers. Some examples of flowers with good color retention after drying are listed below. If you're in doubt as to what will grow in your climate, inquire at your local nursery.

Your Dried Flower Garden

PURPLE/BLUE:
Caspia
Delphinium (Larkspur)
Eryngium (Echinops)
Hydrangea
Lavendula (Lavender)
Mint flowers
Oreganum (Oregano flowers)
Salvia

YELLOW:
Achillea filipendulina (Yarrow)
Dahlia
Helianthus (Sunflower)
Helichrysum (Strawflower)
Lonas inodora
Many roses, including *Rosa*
  'Golden Time'
Sanfordii

ORANGE:
Carthamus (Safflower)
Helichrysum (Strawflower)
Physalis (Chinese lantern)

RED:
Amaranthus
Celosia (Cockscomb)
Gomphrena (Globe amaranth)
Helichrysum (Strawflower)
Pepperberries
Many roses, including *Rosa*
  'Mercedes'

PINK:
Delphinium (Larkspur)
Gomphrena (Globe amaranth)
Heather
Helichrysum (Strawflower)
Hydrangea
Paeonia 'Dr. Flemming' (Dark
  pink peony)
Paeonia 'Sarah Bernhardt'
  (Pink peony)
Pepperberries
Many roses, including *Rosa*
  'Europa' and 'Kiss'

WHITE:
Achillea 'The Pearl'
Ammobium
Anaphalis
Gypsophila (Baby's breath)
Ixodia alta (Australian daisy)
Many roses, including *Rosa*
  'Tineke'

FORAGING IN THE WOODS
If you are fortunate enough to
have woods in your yard, a boun-
ty of materials is available for the
picking. Some examples are:
Acorns
Bittersweet berries
Cattails
Grasses
Milkweed pods
Pinecones
Queen Anne's lace
Sweet gumballs

AIR DRYING

Although there are many techniques for drying flowers, the easiest is air drying. All the flowers cited can be air-dried by following these simple steps:

1. After the morning dew has burned off, select flowers that are at their peak. Certain flowers such as *Helichrysum* (strawflower) must be picked and hung as soon as the heads begin to bloom. If picked too late, the flowers will continue to open as they dry, yielding an unattractive, overdeveloped blossom. Lavender, salvia, and heather also benefit from early picking, as their fragile blooms will fall from the stems as the flowers mature.

2. Cut flowers with the desired amount of stem, removing lower leaves. Trim any damaged or unattractive areas with scissors.

3. Gather flowers in bunches and secure with rubber bands or raffia. Flowers with multiple blossoms such as lavender, delphinium, and heather can be bundled in 8- to 10-stem bunches. Flowers with a single large bloom such as peonies and roses or with large delicate blooms like hydrangeas dry better in small bunches (2 to 6 stems, depending on the size of the flower).

4. Hang bunches upside down on a wall or clothesline indoors. For best results, pick a room that is dark, dry, and well ventilated. A spare closet or dimly lit attic works well, too.

5. The bunches will be dry and ready to use in four to seven days.

Designing with Dried Flowers

ARRANGEMENTS

To make an arrangement, select a basket, pot, or other container and fill with oasis floral foam (found in floral supply and craft stores). Cover the floral foam with sheet moss and insert the flowers in the desired pattern. It is best to "sketch out" the arrangement with greenery first and then add bunches or individual flowers until the container is full.

TOPIARIES

To make a topiary, select a straight branch to use as the "stem." Press a Styrofoam ball onto one end of the stick, and secure with hot glue. Next, sink the other end of the "stem" into a pot partially filled with floral foam. Verify that the stick is perpendicular, then pour plaster of Paris into the pot. The floral foam not only secures the stick but also keeps the pot from cracking as the plaster of Paris dries. Wait about 24 hours until the plaster has set.

With a hot-glue gun, glue sheet moss over the Styrofoam ball. Then glue flowers in a pleasing pattern onto the moss-covered ball. Alternatively, cover the ball with nuts, pinecones, or berries. To finish, cover the hardened plaster in the pot with sheet moss. Glue in place. If desired, tie a wired ribbon to the branch.

WREATHS
A quick and easy method for making wreaths is to start with a simple grapevine wreath (sold in craft stores). Arrange the flowers, leaves, pinecones, and berries on the wreath. Once satisfied with the pattern you have designed, use a hot-glue gun to secure the materials to the base. A French wired ribbon in complementary colors can add an elegant touch.

TIPS
A few suggestions to keep your dried flowers beautiful:
- Spray arrangements with hairspray to preserve them.
- Avoid direct sunlight to keep colors from fading.
- Avoid humidity; moisture causes wilting and fading.
- Use a feather duster or hairdryer on a low setting to keep arrangements dust-free.
- To store unused dried flowers, wrap bunches in tissue paper and place in cardboard cartons in a dark, dry place.
- Experiment, and have fun!

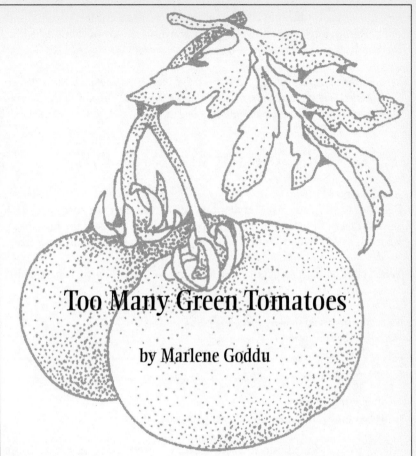

Too Many Green Tomatoes

by Marlene Goddu

Ah, first frost, the bane of northern tomato growers. What to do? Pick them green and coax them into a slow, dark, paper-bag ripening . . . Or, respect the fruit for what it is. But alas, the green forbidden fruit as it stands—shiny, firm, and acidic—the taste raw and flat, needs mothering. My remedy? Cook some love into it.

Where to begin? The obvious, of course, made famous by the movie of the same name.

FRIED GREEN TOMATOES

Slice the tomatoes fairly thick and dip into buttermilk. Make a combination of equal parts cornmeal and flour. Season with kosher salt and pepper to taste.

Fry in hot bacon fat if available, or any oil of your choice, turning only once. Remove to paper towels. Keep warm in the oven while finishing the batch.

Served with bacon and eggs, it's a natural, because the bacon fat is perfect for frying. Fried green tomatoes also make an excellent sandwich layered with bacon and cheese on homemade bread.

GREEN TOMATO SALSA

Roast 4 ears of corn:
Remove all silk and husk, leaving one layer to protect the corn. Peel back the last layer of husk, moisten the corn with water, and fold the husk back. Roast in a 350° oven for approximately half an hour, depending on size.

When cool enough to handle, cut the corn off the cob with a sharp knife.

To this add:
4 green tomatoes, seeded and chopped
½ red onion, chopped
2 tbsp lime juice
2 tbsp chopped fresh cilantro
1 tbsp honey
Kosher salt, to taste
Crushed green, pink, and black peppercorns, to taste

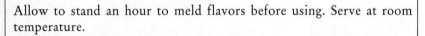

Allow to stand an hour to meld flavors before using. Serve at room temperature.

GREEN TOMATO PIE WITH RED SALAD

This has one of those "in-between" tastes—not a dessert, but not an entrée. Paired with a "red" salad, it makes a unique offering for a garden lunch.

6 to 8 tomatoes
Ritz cracker crumbs
Light brown sugar
Salt

Melted butter
¼ cup heavy cream
1 egg yolk
Pie crust

Slice the tomatoes as thinly as possible. Layer in an uncooked pie shell until the bottom is covered. Sprinkle with about 1 tbsp Ritz cracker crumbs, 1 tsp light brown sugar, ¼ tsp salt, and 1 tbsp melted butter. Make as many of these layers as your pie pan (or your tomatoes) will allow.

Top with pie crust, and make slits for the steam to escape. Create a hole in the center of the pie by pushing your thumb through. Combine the heavy cream and egg yolk, and pour into the hole.

Bake at 350°, for about an hour and let stand for 15–20 minutes before serving. Provide cheese on top if desired.

RED SALAD

The Red Salad can be anything you like to create the reverse of a green salad: red leaf lettuce, red peppers, red cabbage, red onion, and radishes. Dress with:

RUBY BEET AND RED WINE VINAIGRETTE

Wash 2 or 3 beets and cook in boiling, salted water until very soft.

When cool enough to handle, peel and slice into a food processor.

Purée, adding a little beet water to make a smooth paste.

Add to processor:
2 cups olive oil
1 cup red wine vinegar
½ tsp salt
1 tsp sugar
1 tsp Dijon mustard
2 tbsp sour cream

Drizzle this on your salad, and you'll be famous.

Variations on Pesto

by Marlene Goddu

The spinach crop has tripled overnight and spinach salad has gotten too much billing. Sautéed spinach, again? Yawn. Looking for a simple quick alternative . . . without cooking?

Pesto! A practical solution to garden surpluses. These tasty pastes are so easy to make and convenient to use. Pesto can be added to a simple vinaigrette, stew, soup, pasta, orzo, risotto, or rice. It's a great spread on a pizza shell or French bread, or mixed with cream cheese for a dip. Add it to sautéed scallops or broiled sole, stew with some clams, stuff inside pounded chicken breasts, and roast tomatoes or squash topped with it.

Here are a few examples; however, make it your personal statement, and feel free to substitute any herb, oil, or nut. Interchange the ingredients with anything you have too much of; it's hard to go wrong. You need never be bored in the kitchen again!

SPINACH-MACADAMIA PESTO

Combine in food processor:
4 cups uncooked spinach
6 large garlic cloves
1 ½ cups macadamia nuts

While combining, slowly add:
1 ½ cups olive oil

Return to bowl, and stir in:
1 ½ cups Parmesan cheese
Kosher salt and pepper, to taste

PARSLEY-CHIVE-ALMOND PESTO

Combine in food processor:
4 cups parsley, washed thoroughly
1 cup chives
1 cup toasted almonds
1 tbsp fresh thyme
6 large garlic cloves

While combining, slowly add:
1 cup olive oil

Return to bowl, and stir in:
1 cup Parmesan cheese
1 cup chicken stock
Kosher salt and pepper, to taste

Compound Butters

Compound butters are another delicious but simple way to flavor your food. Any combination is possible; mistakes are impossible! So have fun with these and make them your kitchen "staples." You'll breeze through everyday cooking, barbecues, and formal entertaining alike.

SPINACH AND APRICOT COMPOUND BUTTER

In a food processor, combine:
3 cups uncooked spinach
2 cups dried apricots
½ cup sunflower seeds, toasted
2 tsp pink peppercorns

Add:
½ lb softened butter

Form into a tube using plastic wrap, and store until needed.

Slice onto grilled beef, lamb, pork, chicken, or fish. Try the same formula substituting sun-dried cherries and hazelnuts or sun-dried cranberries and almonds.

BRIE AND ROSEMARY COMPOUND BUTTER

In a food processor, combine:
1 lb Brie, with rind removed
½ lb butter

Add:
¼ cup fresh rosemary
1 tbsp pink peppercorns
2 tbsp honey

Form into a tube using plastic wrap, and store until needed. This is excellent sliced onto grilled lamb or chicken.

Making It Through the Winter

by Jan Hack

Raspberry jams glistening in faceted jars; blueberry marmalade scented with cinnamon and a squeeze of lemon; nut-brown peach butter thick and sweet. With these homemade preserves lining your shelves, you're all ready for a long winter. As the holidays approach, others frantically shop for useless, expensive, and impersonal trinkets to present the mail carrier, the teacher, and the hairdresser. While they trudge through the slush and cold, you could be at home, serenely tying bows around homemade jams and chutneys in front of the fire. Why make preserves? Peace of mind!

Here are some guidelines to consider when stocking your own larder.

1. Always use produce that looks ripe, feels heavy and smells of its own essence; bruised or underripe fruit will never get the desired result (epiphanic memories of summer!) no matter how much sugar or herbs are added to your recipe.

2. Prepare your kitchen! Jars should be washed thoroughly and sterilized in a hot-water bath. A hot-water bath is a large kettle filled with enough water to cover the lids of your jars by at least an inch. It is a good idea to put a wire rack under the jars inside the kettle so that they are not in direct contact with the heat source. To sterilize, wash the jars, place them into the filled kettle, and cover. Bring the water to a boil, and leave boiling for 15 minutes. The timing starts after you see steam escaping from below the lid. To process, place filled jars in the same hot water, cover the kettle, and return the water to a boil. Again, timing starts after you see steam escaping from below the lid. For the recipe below, the jars should be processed for 10 minutes.

3. The jars must remain hot until filled, so leave them in the water until your preserves are cooked. Lids can be added to the bath after the sterilization, but not before—they should not be boiled.

4. Tongs for lifting the jars, a funnel for filling the jars, a magnetic wand to fish lids out from the bath, and a cloth for rim wiping should all be at the ready.

5. While most preserves and chutneys require substantial time on the stove, be careful not to overcook or burn the mixture. The recipes should also never be doubled—this only encourages uneven cooking. If you would like to prepare multiple batches, do so in separate pots.

6. If you are not using a commercial pectin (which aids the jelling process), for low-pectin fruits (usually those without stones) it's a good idea to put apple slices in the pot to help boost the pectin content. These are discarded when the jam has finished cooking. Unsure if the recipe has jelled? Place a spoonful on a plate in the freezer for 5 minutes. If it appears thick, it's done!

7. Make sure to choose appropriate-size jars. Twelve ounces of chutney is usually plenty; a larger container will only encourage spoilage once it is open. Conversely, the 4-ounce jar generally provides only one or two servings. Most important, all jars and bands regardless of size should be in perfect condition. They may be reused, but lids (as distinct from bands) must be purchased new each time.

RASPBERRY JAM

12 cups clean raspberries, picked over
4 cups sugar
Juice of ½ lemon
1 apple, quartered (seeds and all)
1 cup water

Bring all ingredients to a boil, and then lower to a simmer, stirring occasionally. Check the consistency after half an hour. It should be fairly thick—like sour cream. When done, ladle the mixture into sterilized jars (discarding the apples), wipe the rim, and close with lids and bands. These filled jars can then be processed in the hot-water bath for 10 minutes. This should yield approximately 6 half-pint jars.

Gifts from the Garden

by Elizabeth L. Haskins

Nothing is better than a homemade gift, unless it is a gift made from the bounty of your own garden! Try the following gift ideas at holiday time when you can make them in batches. And remember, your presentation will make all the difference. Creatively wrap the gifts in colored tissue paper or a lovely cotton. Make a beautiful card with recipe hints or instructions and tie it around the jars or bottles with ribbon or decorative cord. Or use an unusual rubber stamp (I use a starfish) to print your own special labels. But most of all, enjoy the process.

HERBED MUSTARD

8 oz jar of Dijon mustard
1 tsp minced oregano
2 tsp minced thyme
1 tsp minced tarragon

In a bowl, mix the mustard and herbs to taste. Return to the original jar or a decorative jar with a tight stopper. Refrigerate for 2–3 weeks before serving.

CITRUS MUSTARD

If you have citrus trees, make citrus mustard by substituting the herbs for 2 tsp each of freshly grated lemon and orange zest and 2 tsp of lemon thyme.

And if you are a purist and would like to make your own mustard . . .

Add to a food processor:
8 oz mustard powder
2 tbsp sugar
2 tsp salt
6 oz cider vinegar

Process the ingredients until the sugar has dissolved, and then slowly and in a steady stream add 6 oz of olive oil until it is incorporated. Remove from the processor and stir in the desired herbs or citrus flavoring.

BERRY VINEGAR

1½ cups fresh, washed raspberries, blackberries, or strawberries
6 cups good-quality white wine vinegar
½ cup sugar
Quart jar or bottle with a tight lid

Once the berries are dry, add them to the jar or bottle. Over low heat, warm the vinegar and sugar, stirring until the sugar dissolves. Remove from heat and add to the berry bottle, slightly mashing the berries to release their flavor. Seal the bottle and set aside for 2 weeks in a dark, cool place. Strain and pour into decorative bottles or jars. For a prettier presentation, add fresh berries to the jars.

HERBED VINEGAR

To make herbed vinegars, place your own combination of herbs in a decorative bottle, warm a good-quality white wine vinegar, and pour it into the decorative bottles. Try herbs such as rosemary, French tarragon, basil, dill, and thyme. Flavor them with garlic; red, green, and black peppercorns; chile peppers; and strips of citrus peels. Use a tried and true combination such as rosemary and garlic, or concoct your own recipe using the harvest from your own garden.

HERBES DE PROVENCE

Herbes de Provence is a blend of herbs used in southern France to flavor a variety of dishes. Create your own balance of dried marjoram, oregano, rosemary, sage, and thyme. Fill in small glass jars with a decorative label. Include a recipe card with a classic Provençal dish.

MANY-BEAN SOUP

There are a number of different packages of bean soups available on the market, but you can make your own using your own dried herbs and a creative presentation. This is a good gift for cooking enthusiasts, who will take this basic recipe and make it their own.

1. The first step is to fill the jars with the beans. You will need:

> 2 cups of 5 different dried beans (such as lentils, cannellini beans, split peas, cranberry beans, or black-eyed peas)
> 2 cups pearl barley
> 3 canning or other decorative jars (½ quart)

When you select the dried beans, look for beautiful beans or go for a striking color combination. Divide the beans and barley between the 3 jars, layering the different varieties. (Or you can mix them all together and then fill the jars.) Close the jars.

2. The next step is to make a packet of spices. Use your own dried herbs, such as thyme, bay leaves, sage, parsley, and oregano, and package them in little bundles of cheesecloth or small decorated gift envelopes.

3. Include a recipe card for the soup. Adapt one of your own or use the basic recipe below:

> 4 cloves garlic
> 2 medium onions
> 1 large carrot
> 1 large celery stalk
> 5 tbsp olive oil
> 4 quarts water or chicken broth

- Wash the dried beans and barley and let them dry in a colander.
- Mince the vegetables and garlic. In a large soup kettle, sauté them with the herbs or herb bundle for about 6–7 minutes or until the vegetables are soft.
- Add the dried beans and barley and sauté, stirring constantly, for another minute or so.
- Add the water or chicken broth and cover.
- Simmer (1½ hours or so), adding water or broth as necessary, until the beans are soft.
- Season with salt. Serve drizzled with extra-virgin olive oil and an offering of freshly ground pepper and Parmesan cheese.

4. Gather the jar of beans, the spice packet or bundle, and the recipe card and wrap in tissue paper or cellophane or tie the three together with ribbon.

ROSE PETAL JAM

If you have an abundance of roses, you may feel it is worthwhile to sacrifice a few of your most fragrant for this delicious jelly. But only do so if you grow your roses without the use of pesticides.

> 20 roses cut at their prime
> 6 cups sugar
> 5 cups water
> ½ tsp citric acid

Remove the petals from the roses, tearing in half those that are large, and place in a large bowl. Heat the sugar in 4 cups water until it has dissolved, then boil for an additional half hour. Meanwhile, boil the last cup of water in a separate pot and add to the bowl with the rose petals. Stir, then pour into the boiling sugar and water mixture. Continue to boil, all the while stirring to keep the petals from rising to the surface. In half an hour or so, when the liquid is clear, add the citric acid. Boil for approximately 10 minutes more or until the liquid turns to a clear thickened syrup. Pour into prepared jars and seal.

LAVENDER SOAP

6 tbsp grated castile soap
1 pint water
5 tbsp glycerine
5 drops lavender

Put soap and water in a double boiler and heat. When the soap has melted, add the glycerine. Stir and remove from the heat. Add the lavender drops, let cool, and pour into clean bottles. Seal with a tight cork or cap.

ROSEMARY OR LAVENDER BATH SACHETS

Muslin
Decorative ribbon
Oatmeal
Powdered milk
Dried rosemary or lavender

Make a little bag with the muslin, sewing up three sides. In a large bowl mix together like amounts of the powdered milk and oatmeal, adding enough dried rosemary or lavender to scent the mixture. Fill the muslin bags, trim the top with pinking shears, and secure with ribbon.

LAVENDER PILLOW

Lavender, known for its affinity with a woman's spirit, was traditionally tied in bundles and put in the hands of women going through labor. During the Middle Ages, sprigs of lavender were said to calm hysteria. Offer a lavender-scented pillow to soothe a soul and relieve tension and stress to the eyes.

Make a small square pillow case out of cheesecloth or muslin, sewing up three sides. Stuff with dried lavender and hem shut. Make a pretty case, only slightly larger, of a light cotton or soft linen, sewing up three sides and using a drawstring, buttons, or snaps on the fourth. (This will make it easier to replace the lavender when the fragrance is gone.) Put the small muslin case inside.

HERBED BATH OILS

Almond or apricot kernel oil
Sprigs of rosemary or lavender
Small glass decanters

Fill the decanters with either almond or apricot kernel oil and add sprigs of rosemary or lavender. Keep on a sunny windowsill for a few weeks to let the warmth of the sun release the scent of the herbs. This makes a very special and personal gift, particularly if you are lucky enough to find a lovely old perfume decanter.

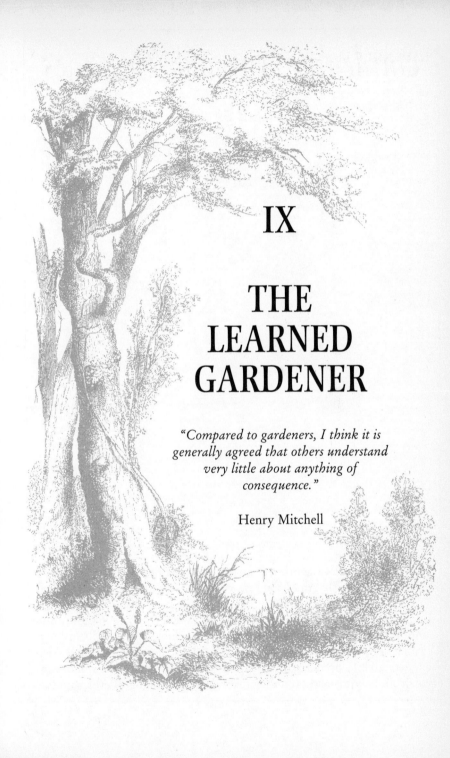

IX

THE
LEARNED
GARDENER

*"Compared to gardeners, I think it is
generally agreed that others understand
very little about anything of
consequence."*

Henry Mitchell

Gardening Through the Ages

by Eric Swanson

Survival was the primary goal of America's first settlers. Probably for this reason, early American history has a great deal to say about vegetables and precious little about landscape art. Near the end of the 17th century, improved economic conditions allowed an interest in beauty and comfort to arise, and citizens of Colonial townships such as Williamsburg, Virginia, responded by erecting public gardens. These were simple, rectangular affairs, dominated by hardy shrubs like box hedge and yew, which could withstand even the most relentless pruning. (Perhaps to fulfill a psychological need to impose order on a largely wild landscape, early Colonial gardeners enjoyed few things more than whacking shrubbery into precise, geometric shapes.) Imported tulips, crocuses, and lilies, along with native varieties of violets and wild asters, provided spots of color among the hedges. Individual householders, meanwhile, planted kitchen gardens, bordered by sweet or tangy herbs for flavoring their food. Serious herbalists grew honeysuckle, lavender, marigolds, and poppies and distilled the juices of these flowers for medicinal purposes.

During this same period, inquisitive souls began to look with wonder on the interesting plant life all around them, and amateur and professional botanists began recording examples of native flora and transplanting specimens into their private gardens. A gentleman farmer named John Bartram established the first botanical garden on his farm near Philadelphia, and he traveled as far north as Lake Erie and as far south as Florida to gather specimens. His wife thought his expeditions a wee bit eccentric; fortunately for the sake of botanical science, she expired before she could dissuade him. Bartram's achievements inspired many of his contemporaries to follow his example, and lush botanical gardens sprang up across the Atlantic seaboard.

In the 18th century, wealthy American landowners—like their European counterparts—began building splendid homes for themselves. They hired French and British landscape artists to plant sweeping geometric mazes of persistently popular shrubbery punctuated by small symmetrical beds of roses, poppies, tulips, and lilies. These elaborate designs were meant to extend the architecture of the estate, according to the Renaissance Italian theory that "things planted should reflect things built." A few humble householders caught the gardening spirit as well, and though vegetable gardens remained a fixture of ordinary Colonial homes, purely decorative beds gained a bit more real estate.

Toward the end of the 18th century, Europe's formal gardens were being replanted in a more naturalistic, or romantic, design based on sweeping lawns, gently rising hills, and rivers and ponds accented by informal clumps of trees and—of course—shrubbery. Thomas Jefferson and George Washington, both passionate gardeners, incorporated these softer design elements on their Virginia estates; but the romantic style didn't take hold in America until the middle of the 19th century, when Andrew Jackson Downing, the first great American landscape architect, adapted it to areas along the Hudson River and Long Island, New York. The rambling parks Downing designed on the estates of his clients evoked an idealized image of nature, eminently suitable for long walks and tasteful picnics. Rolling meadows led to artificial ponds or creeks, on whose banks sprang bluebells, daffodils, and other wildflowers, cunningly planted to imitate natural growth. Clumps of largely native trees provided shady areas, while stone bridges, pagodas, and weathered statuary erected at various turnings were meant to surprise the eye. A line of concealed ditches prevented deer or cattle from entering the park and spoiling the grounds with rude activities. Each ditch was called a "ha-ha." The origin of the term is unclear, however, and must be left to the imagination of the reader.

Downing's work was continued by Frederick Law Olmsted, undoubtedly the most famous American landscape architect of the 19th century. In 1854, together with Downing's partner, Calvert Vaux, Olmsted designed New York City's Central Park —the first major public example of landscape architecture in the United States. Out of some 840 acres of swamp, bluff, and rock in the center of Manhattan, Olmsted and Vaux created a naturalistic landscape in the English romantic style, a soothing interplay of light and shade, where sprawling meadows merged seamlessly with picturesque woodlands and formal strolling grounds. To foster an illusion of unbroken expanse, Olmsted and Vaux sank four transverse roads 8 feet below the park's surface to carry crosstown traffic and built separate avenues for carriage drives, pedestrian walks, and equestrian activities. More than 40 bridges managed crossings between the different routes, while stone benches and wooden pagodas provided picturesque rest areas for the weary wanderer. Central Park succeeded so well as both a municipal venture and an artistic creation spawned like endeavors across the country. Olmsted designed many of these public parks himself, including Washington and Jackson Parks in Chicago, Belle Island Park in Detroit, and the grounds of the Capitol in Washington, D.C. His success established landscape architecture as a professional discipline, while his artistic vision inspired an entire generation of public planners.

The years following the Civil War witnessed the sudden expansion of seed companies and plant nurseries, along with the publication of scores of gardening manuals and horticultural journals. Hundreds of new species were imported to the United States from Asia, Africa, and Central and South America; in response to these developments, landscape artists evolved ever more complicated and exotic designs to suit the competitive tastes of their wealthy employers. Depending on one's point of view, the result was either a veritable Persian carpet of intricate patterns or a floral mess.

As the Victorian age drew to a close, women seized control of the American gardening scene. In 1890 a group of wealthy Georgian ladies founded the Athens Garden Club as a forum for exchanging ideas and experiences. The movement spread to other cities, culminating in 1913 with the birth of the Garden Club of America in Philadelphia. Its members hoped to foster interest in home beautification among all classes of American society, and through their efforts garden clubs soon sprang up in great numbers across the country. The club also undertook civic projects, including wildflower conservation, roadside planting, and the preservation of the Pacific redwood forest. Smaller garden clubs, meanwhile, sponsored flower shows, which served to ignite local interest in home gardening; in short order, rectangular beds of hollyhocks, phlox, azaleas, and roses, neatly arranged inside hedges or fences, became a staple ornament of the American suburban home. In 1924, garden associations across New York State joined together to form the first Federated Garden Club, under the direction of Louise Beebe Wylder, who eventually became a director of the New York Botanical Garden. Wylder's passion for rock gardens and tiny alpine flowers such as the ox-eye daisy, the buttercup, and the spring crocus inspired many alpine gardens across the country.

During the first decades of the 20th century, American designers flirted with the Beaux-Arts style, characterized by flower beds laid out in soft, undulating lines, often referred to as whiplash lines. By the 1930s, however, modernist ideas had begun to infiltrate garden design. Architects such as Frank Lloyd Wright broke down the distinction between indoor and outdoor spaces, using simple, fluid designs to harmonize or to repeat patterns in the natural environment. In areas with mild climates, such as California, gardens were extended from the yard into the house, through the careful deployment of glass walls and ingenious planters. From California as well came the next wave of 20th-century garden aesthetics, as designers for the silver screen reinterpreted the Spanish patio as the ideal setting for glamorous parties and romantic interludes. Soon abstract groupings of tropical plants and exotic flowers began to grace the patios of Hollywood homes; owing largely to Hollywood's influence on the American psyche, patios became a popular adjunct to millions of American homes, and the traditional suburban garden became an outside room, a comfortable space for entertaining, relaxation, and occasional infidelities.

During the latter half of the 20th century, increased familiarity with other cultures generated a broad range of popular garden designs. Presently, we see re-creations of Italian Renaissance gardens, complete with fountains, stone cherubs, and brightly colored flowers interspersed with secret "rooms" of evergreen shrubbery. Zen gardens provide a soothing spot for meditation among graceful bonsai, careful rock formations, blocks of irises, and perhaps a deep green pond dressed with floating lilies. While the grand, formal designs of the 18th century have been resurrected in such places as Williamsburg and the Sonnenberg Gardens in upstate New York, at the other end of the scale, informal English cottage gardens, profusely planted with hardy flowers and bulbs and low hedges, have also enjoyed a surge of popularity. In many major urban areas, meanwhile, lavish botanical gardens recall the scientific pursuits of two centuries ago.

Several noted designers have abandoned European influences altogether and developed a distinctively American approach to landscape gardening. Thomas Church, author of the influential book *Gardens for People,* rejected the hoary notion of a garden as a work of art and created gardens as practical extensions of a house, where people could work, entertain, or relax. He outlined the boundaries of each outdoor "room" with stone and concrete and planted them with indigenous flora, which would not require a great deal of effort to maintain. Church designed exclusively in California, where weather conditions permit living and working outdoors. In parts of the country where snow, sleet, and occasional hailstorms inhibit most sane people from throwing a pool party in December, designers have necessarily adapted some of his ideas. Jens Jensen, in the Midwest, planted wide, variegated fields of prairie grasses; Wolfgang Oehme and James Van Sweden, in the Northeast, have likewise made use of grasses and other local plant material to create somewhat idealized versions of an American meadow. Reductions in the traditional domestic workforce, meanwhile, and the expansion of leisure industries have given rise to a need for more-functional home gardens. Small plots have now become the norm, planted with flowers that require relatively simple care, such as coreopsis, cleome, and achillea.

Recent concern for the environment brings the history of American gardening full circle. So-called green groups have, for example, revitalized many abandoned urban areas through the planting of community gardens, while at the same time individual homeowners have begun to take pride in growing their own vegetables without chemical fertilizers or insecticides. A deeper understanding of the effects of human interaction with the environment has brought home to many people the importance of preserving the balance of nature. Thus, like the first wave of settlers in the New World, modern American gardeners have by necessity become engaged in the rough business of survival. Whether we know it or not, every plant we grow strikes a blow not only for our own gardens but for the vast, common garden of humankind as well.

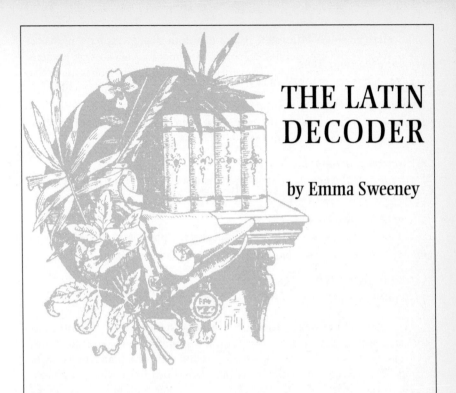

THE LATIN DECODER

by Emma Sweeney

The internationally accepted method for naming plants is the Latin binomial system, which, like the Latin you may remember from high school, follows clear, specific rules. What looks complicated and overwhelming can readily be understood once you know the formula:

- All plants have a genus name in italics, which comes first and tells you the plant's genus or type (a noun).
- A species name in italics follows the genus (an adjective describing the noun).
- The presence of a third name in italics denotes that the plant is a subspecies (designated ssp.) or naturally occurring variety (var.).
- A roman multiplication sign (✕) indicates a hybrid (the crossing of two genera, species, or cultivars).
- A capitalized name in roman in single quotation marks indicates the plant is a cultivar, a *cultivated variety* usually named by the person who propagated the plant.

Here are a few "decoded" Latin names of plants:

Hydrangea arborescens
Hydrangea is the name of the genus; *arborescens* is the name of species.

Hydrangea arborescens radiata
Hydrangea is the name of the genus, *arborescens* is the name of species, and here *radiata* is the subspecies.

Hydrangea macrophylla 'Mariesii'
Hydrangea is the genus, *macrophylla* the species, and 'Mariesii' the name of this cultivar within the *macrophylla* species.

Clematis × *jouiniana*
Clematis is the genus and the "×" indicates the plant is a hybrid between two species, in this case *jouiniana*.

Clematis 'Jackmanii'
Clematis is the genus and *Jackmanii* is the name of this cultivar.

Botanical Latin is a richly descriptive system that is both informative and useful, particularly when you are shopping for a specific plant, because a genus can be quite large. If you don't know a plant by its Latin name, you may end up with the wrong plant. For instance, if you go to a nursery and order a "hydrangea," you could get a climbing hydrangea (*Hydrangea anomala* ssp. *petiolaris*), a shrub (*H. macrophylla*) or even a tree, the peegee hydrangea (*H. paniculata*). However, if you know you want *Hydrangea quercifolia*, you will get oakleaf hydrangea, which is very different from the other hydrangeas.

The species names can tell you a lot about the plants themselves: *quercifolia*, (*querci*,oak; *folia*, leaf), *anomala* (out of the ordinary), *paniculata* (having flowers borne in a cluster). By decoding these names, you can learn about the plant's shape, the color and size of its flowers and foliage, the plant's origins (species *texanus* came from Texas, *tibeticus* from Tibet). You can even sometimes learn how a plant smells, as in the adjective *foetidus* ("bad smelling" for example, *Iris foetidissima*).

While these polysyllabic Latin words may seem unwieldy at first, you might take solace in the fact that there are no hard-and-fast rules as to the correct pronunciation. The American Horticultural Society provides suggestions for pronouncing them, but in some cases proper pronunciation goes to the "you say po-tay-to, I say po-tah-to" argument.

Try to use Latin nomenclature for plants as often as possible. Once you've decoded the words, you'll be glad to know what they mean and to address your plants by their proper names.

THE BOTANY LESSON

by Eric Swanson

Characters of the dialogue:
Epistamos, a tutor
Ganymede, a young scholar

Epistamos: Ganymede, let us linger beneath this olive tree while you rehearse the main points of yesterday's lesson. First, what is the dominant form of plant life on earth?

Ganymede: The dominant form of plant life is called angiosperm, which means "enclosed seed," because the seed is protected within the plant. Flowering plants, shrubs, herbs, and many trees are included in this category. Fir trees, cycads, and ginkgoes, whose seeds lie exposed on the surface of hard cones, belong to the class Gymnospermae, which I believe refers to their athletic prowess.

Epistamos: Correct until the last point. "Gymnosperm" means "naked seed." Pray now, what are the principal organs of both classes?

Ganymede: The three principal organs of both angiosperm and gymnosperm are the root, the stem, and the leaf. The root grows downward, anchoring the plant in the soil, while drawing water and nutrients up to feed the stem and leaves. The stem of most plants grows vertically above ground, although some creep along the surface of the soil, while others, such ivy, attach to vertical surfaces such as tree trunks, walls, or decorative trellises. Leaves spring from nodes along the stem and consist of loosely arranged cells, which absorb carbon dioxide from the air, expel oxygen, and change the light of the sun into food through a process called photography.

Epistamos: "Photosynthesis" is the correct term.

Ganymede: Thank you, sir. To continue, most leaves are flat or bladelike. Some develop as spines or thorns, which protect the plant from predators. Others are colored, to encourage insects to visit small or uncomely flowers. Flowers are the most highly specialized type of leaves.

Epistamos: Excellent! Let us proceed to more serious matters. How do angiosperm reproduce?

Ganymede: Propagation is carried out by flowers, which consist of four sections arranged in separate series. The tough, outer series are called sepals, which protect the bud before it opens. Next come petals, which attract pollinators such as bees and butterflies by means of their gay colors and minute secretions of fragrant oils. Within the petals can be seen one or two circles of male reproductive organs, called stamens, which produce grains of pollen. In the very center of the flower stands the pistil, the female reproductive organ, which has three sections. The base is called an ovary, where egg cells are produced. A tube, or style, rises up from the ovary and is capped by a mouthlike opening called the stigma. When grains of pollen are introduced into the stigma, they travel down the style to the ovary and merge with the egg cells. This fusion creates seeds, tiny plant embryos protected and fed by a thin layer of surrounding tissues. Seeds are often embedded in a thicker layer of tissue, which can be used to make pies or side dishes.

Epistamos: Intelligent boy! Now, do flowers fertilize themselves, or is another agent necessary?

Ganymede: Zeus in His wisdom has ordered the male and female organs of each plant of a given species to develop at different times. Exceptions to the rule can be found, however, because Zeus in His infinite wisdom has left room for errors in timing. In most cases, though, biological agents, such as birds or insects, or environmental agents, such as wind, are required to carry pollen from the mature stamen of one plant to the mature pistil of another. In this way, the characteristics of parent plants are combined haphazardly to produce more-diverse offspring, which may better adapt to changes in the environment.

Epistamos: I am pleased by your recitation, Ganymede. Have you any questions?

Ganymede: Only one, sir.

Epistamos: Proceed.

Ganymede: Learned tutor, I have located on my person a structure that I believe to be a stamen. I am curious, however, to discover the whereabouts of my pistil.

Epistamos: The answer to your question lies beyond the scope of the present lesson, I fear. Let us withdraw to the house for a meal replete with tempting side dishes and delicious pies.

Ganymede: Willingly, good master, as hummingbirds to fragrant blossoms fly.

How to
Talk Green

by Susan Dooley

Where once the cocktail circuit buzzed with the culinary ABC's of arugula, bruschetta, and cassoulet, now it is achillea, balsam, and chives. America has gone into the garden, and social survival depends on learning how to talk green. Since gardeners love Latin almost as much as they love the earth they work in, you can make an immediate impression by quoting Virgil.

> Yet sprinkle sordid ashes all around,
> And load with fattening dung thy fallow ground.
> Thus change of seeds for meagre soils is best;
> And earth manured, not idle, though at rest.

It is better if you can render this in the original Latin. But if you have trouble committing that much Virgil to memory, you can still impress with a single phrase: genius loci. This "genius of the place" is the god who presides over each little bit of land, and a mention makes gardeners quite mystical. This phrase doesn't mean anything, but the listener will think it does.

You can also impress with a bit of gardening history, which is exactly like the history of sexual mores. One generation lets loose the stays and indulges in blowsiness in the beds. The next tightens up the corset and forces everything back into line.

When led through the paths and parterres of a formal garden, say, "How Le Nôtre endures," this being the name of the 17th-century French landscape architect who created Versailles. You may then add, "You do know that he hated flowers?"

When the vista is dominated by trees and grass, the name to drop is Capability Brown, an 18th-century landscaper who took the garden back to nature, transplanting entire groves of trees and inserting lakes and streams where none had been before. His followers went a step further. Giving in to a loony romanticism, they built ready-made ruins, erected hermitages, and vainly sought to employ hermits to live in them.

Naturally, the gardeners of the 19th-century felt compelled to reassert control with a practice known as "bedding out." Not sexual laxity—these were Victorians, remember—but a way of ensuring that when you wanted a pink petunia, you got one. Gardeners took the gamble out of gardening by growing their plants out of sight. When the flowers had burst into bloom, they were trotted over to the garden and put where they belonged. Bedding out gave the gardener a chance to arrange low-growing annuals in such a way that the observer might mistake them for Persian carpets, American flags, or fallen neon signs.

The reaction against bedding out was the cottage garden, a blowsy blend of old roses, forgotten perennials, and colorful annuals championed by Gertrude Jekyll. Pronounce it *JEE-ckle,* and raise a disdainful eyebrow at anyone who dares to pair Gertrude Jekyll with Mr. Hyde.

Remember that ladybugs are good, cucumber beetles bad. That once it was socially unacceptable to have bats in your belfry; now it is mandatory and garden catalogs offer special houses for these creatures that keep mosquitoes at bay. Before you lower your bottom to a bench, look critically at the gardener and ask if it is made of plantation teak, while muttering about the ruin of the rain forest. And if you want to dish the dirt, smirk at the nearby border and confide that "Mrs. Sinkins is very good in bed with the Prime Minister."

Don't forget to pronounce the "h" in "herbs," accent the second syllable of "clematis" and insist on calling your pruning shears secateurs.

If all this seems too much trouble, you can convince your gardening friends that you are a person of horticultural knowledge and superior taste by simply saying, "You have made an Eden here on earth."

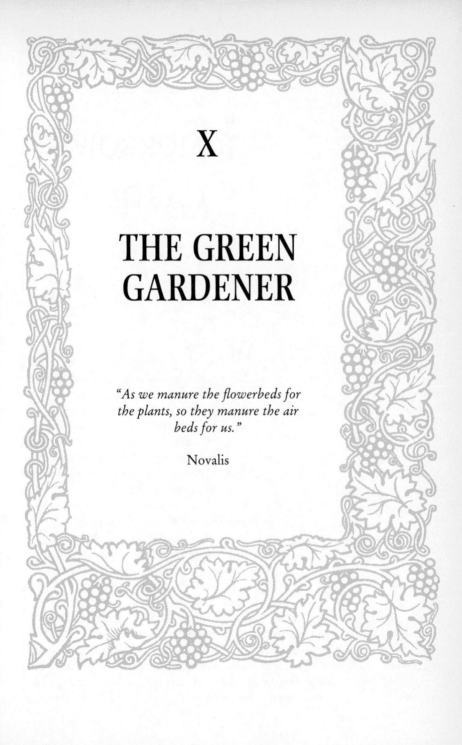

X

THE GREEN GARDENER

"As we manure the flowerbeds for the plants, so they manure the air beds for us."

Novalis

TOMORROW'S GARDEN

by Ken Druse

We've all heard of global warming. That's primarily the result of burning fossil fuel, which increases the levels of carbon dioxide in the atmosphere. (Another cause is the destruction of tropical rain forests, still slashed and burned at the rate of 30 million acres a year.) If current consumption continues, the level of carbon dioxide could double in the next five years; scientists theorize that the earth's temperature could rise between 6° and 12° F . You don't have to imagine the polar ice cap melting or picture Ohio beachfront to make a startling realization: think of your 1977 air-conditioning bill.

There isn't one clear solution. But shade is at the root of an appealing idea. Trees, especially young trees, gobble up carbon dioxide. And of course as the trees take in contaminants, they spew out their waste product—oxygen. The American Forestry Association, a citizens' group, suggests we plant enough trees over the next several years to slow global warming—reversing the current practice. Today we plant only one tree for every four that are harvested, destroyed, or die of old age.

A tree-planting campaign helps the globe in less direct ways, too. Trees help cut down the consumption of energy. A shade tree is one of the best ways to cool a house, reducing the need for air-conditioning. (A deciduous tree, losing its leaves in winter, will allow the warming sun into the house. Evergreen trees, used as windscreens, can reduce heating costs in the colder months.) The five hottest summers of the 20th-century occurred during the 1980s; in the future, house plans will include shelter from the sun.

The garden of the future will be a shade garden, for all kinds of reasons—fiscal, historical, and, most of all, environmental. It may not grow overnight—but this is a return to an older notion of landscaping, planting for generations to come. It may require a little extra planning, some more thought, more effort—but the knowledge that this small patch contributes to the health of the planet makes it worthwhile. It may not result in masses of frothy color—but there will be color. Just look again at the plants from the forest's floor: they have so little time to gather light, flower, attract pollinators, and set seed that they pack every precious bit of energy into a few spectacular blossoms. Some may seem more grotesque than showy; the plant's energy may not have been put into something we consider "pretty" but into uniqueness. To me, these are the exotic stars of the plant kingdom, destined to become the stars of tommorow's gardens as well. And by the end of our walk in the woods, I trust you too will have come to see shade not as a curse but as a natural opportunity to grow some of the most remarkable botanical wonders of the temperate world.

The Organic Garden: Nature's Symphony

by Wendy Gordon

Eliot Coleman, the renowned organic gardener, aptly compares the skills of a gardener with those of a conductor. "The musicians are all very good at what they do individually. The role of the conductor is not to play each instrument but rather to nurture the union of the disparate parts."

The organic garden works in much the same way as an orchestra. The major players—sun, air, water, soil, microorganisms, fungi, mineral particles—are all part of a system. The role of the gardener is to power this system by nurturing the natural processes, thus enabling them not only to do their job but to excel.

When planning your garden, employ the following "good gardening practices" to support nature's symphony and to allow your garden to flourish.

I. Choose a Good Site

Consider *all* of the following when siting your garden:

SUNSHINE Sunlight is the engine behind photosynthesis. Every effort must be made to take full advantage of it, especially during the early and late months of the growing season.

ASPECT TO THE LAND If possible, sight your garden for southern exposure, which warms up sooner in the spring.

If your land slopes, a southwestern slope is preferable to a southern or southeastern slope. A southwestern slope gets less direct sunlight for dew or frost to evaporate in the early morning. More moisture is available for absorption once the initial daily warming has occurred.

SOIL DEPTH The three factors to consider are the depth of the topsoil, bedrock, and water table. The depth of the topsoil is crucially linked to soil productivity. Fortunately, this factor can be modified over time. Subsoil tillage, deep-rotary tillage, manuring, and the growing of deep-rooted soil-improving crops will all help to increase the depth of your topsoil.

The depth of both the bedrock and the water table, however, can't be changed. When considering the water table, make sure that you look at the land in all seasons. Land that otherwise appears acceptable may have a seasonally high water table, which could make spring planting difficult or impossible.

AIR DRAINAGE Good air circulation in the garden is a must for healthy plants. A low area with stagnant air encourages fungal diseases, holds air pollutants around plants, and stays colder on frosty nights.

Of course, an excessively windy site should also be avoided. It can damage plants, cause wind-borne soil erosion, and create a colder microclimate due to the cooling action of the moving air.

WATER The ideal water supply is a year-round spring or stream that can be tapped into or a dependable pond from which water can be pumped.

II. Know Your Soil

There are three basic types of soil:

Clay consists of fine particles that help the soil hold water and provide a potentially rich storehouse of plant nutrients.

Sand consists of larger particles, mostly silicates, that keep the soil open for air and water penetration and aid early warming in the spring.

Silt falls somewhere between these two.

A fourth soil ingredient—humus or organic matter—is the key to productivity. It opens up heavy clay soils, allowing for better air and water movement and easier working. It also helps hold together and give structure to light sandy soils, creating stabler conditions for the provision of water and nutrients to plants.

Loamy soil is a balance of clay, sand, and silt and is the soil of choice for many plants; the dream soil for most vegetables is a sandy loam. Know your soil, and whenever possible, select plants that are compatible to your type of soil.

III. Build Soil Fertility

Probably 90 percent of all garden failures are caused by poor soil. The attention to soil fertility is the main reason organic gardening produces good results—organic gardening is basically organic soil building.

In a conventional system, the farmer provides plant food in a "predigested" form because the soil fertility is considered inadequate. A symptom—poor plant growth—is treated by using a temporary solution—soluble plant food.

But food for plants does not need to be prearranged in a factory! In an organic system, the soil is supplied with the raw materials needed to produce its own plant food. The aim is to amend the soil to be not only adequate but exceptional.

Build soil fertility by adding the following raw materials to your soil:

ORGANIC MATTER Compost or manure applied every other year.

ROCK PHOSPHATE A finely ground rock powder applied every four years.

GREENSAND MARL An ancient seabed deposit containing some potassium but principally included as a broad-spectrum source of micronutrients. Applied every four years.

LIMESTONE ROCK A ground rock containing calcium and magnesium used to raise the soil pH. Sufficient lime should be applied to keep the pH of your vegetable garden between 6.2 and 6.8.

SPECIFIC MICRONUTRIENTS Elements such as zinc, copper, cobalt, boron, and molybdenum are needed in very small quantities but are absolutely essential for a fertile soil. They will usually be adequately supplied if you have paid attention to pH and organic matter. The need for supplemental applications is best determined through soil tests and plant performance.

IV. Manage Weeds

In an organic garden, managing weeds is done physically, primarily by cultivation, and not chemically. Cultivation is the shallow stirring of the surface soil in order to cut off small weeds and to prevent the appearance of new ones. Don't wait until the weeds are already established; not only will your task become more laborious, but the large weeds will compete with the crop plants for nutrients and water.

V. Manage Pests

The better you furnish the optimum growing conditions for the needs of your plants, the more disease- and pest-resistant your plants will be. Insects and disease are not accidental. They are not a whim of nature. They, too, have their role in the natural system and become destructive only when growing conditions are unfavorable to the crop.

The only dependable remedy to a pest problem is one that aims at correcting the cause. Review your gardening practices. What made your plants vulnerable to infestation? Was the soil properly prepared and amended to meet the needs of the plant? Was there a sufficient supply of water? Was the plant variety you selected suitable not only for your climate but for its spot in the garden? Was the plant set out or sown at the right time? Is there another contributing factor you haven't considered?

A lot can be learned by analyzing the reason for the appearance of pests or the failure of a plant to survive. The end result will be a deeper understanding of the causes and a better-informed course of action in the future.

Organic gardening is not complicated. Nor is it difficult. It is the most straightforward way of raising plants. Difficulties usually arise from a misunderstanding of the gardener's role in the cycle. With sound knowledge and a respect for the processes at work on your property, gardeners from backyard to back forty can tune in to the existing balances of the natural system and give their plants what they need to thrive.

THE EPA'S DO'S AND DON'TS OF LAWN CARE

Careful monitoring and knowledgeable lawn maintenance can prevent the most common lawn-care problems and reduce your need for pesticides and water. Be forewarned: making the transition from chemical treatment of a lawn to natural control may take a couple of years. It takes time to develop healthy soil and a strong root system and to reestablish the natural balance between beneficial organisms and pests in the lawn, but the results can be very rewarding. Here are some "starters."

DO:

CHOOSE NATIVE OR RESISTANT GRASSES

Grass types suited to your climate and light conditions are naturally more resistant to the local pests and diseases. If you prefer other grass types that are not necessarily suited to your environment, choose pest- and disease-resistant varieties.

DEVELOP HEALTHY SOIL

A fistful of healthy soil contains billions of microscopic organisms that break down organic matter and make nutrients available to your grass. Test your soil, adding the recommended nutrients. Organic amendments release nutrients slowly; quick-release chemical fertilizers can brown the grass, induce pest infestations, increase thatch buildup, and promote leaf growth at the expense of healthy root growth.

AERATE THE LAWN

Soil compaction prohibits air and water from reaching the roots of your plants. Aerate your lawn two to three times a year or as needed. While aerating machines can be rented, the best natural aerator is the earthworm. Remember, pesticides can kill or repel earthworms from inhabiting your lawn.

MOW WITH SHARP BLADES

Dull blades can damage the tips of grass, allowing moisture loss and causing it to turn brown. A clean cut stimulates healthy growth.

EXPLORE ALTERNATIVES TO GRASS

Plant grass only in areas that can sustain the proper light and nutrients for good growth. In areas difficult for grass to naturally thrive, plant ground covers, shrubs, and trees; they usually require less maintenance and provide habitats for insect-eating birds.

DON'T:

OVERWATER

Frequent watering wastes water and discourages your grass from developing a deep root system. Water only when necessary and avoid watering in the strong sun or heat—the water will evaporate too quickly and the sun's reflection off the water-laden blade can burn the grass. Also avoid watering at night in areas where the temperature drops markedly in the evenings, because the cool moisture can shock the grass.

MOW THE GRASS TOO SHORT

Mowing too short robs your lawn of food-producing blades of grass, encourages weeds by allowing too much light, and restricts root development of the lawn, making it susceptible to heat, drought, disease, and compaction. The desired height varies according to the grass variety. Keep your mower set on the highest setting if it has one.

ALLOW THATCH BUILD-UP

Thatch is the dense brown layer of grass stems and roots underlying your lawn. In a healthy chemical-free lawn, microorganisms and earthworms decompose thatch and release the nutrients into the soil and roots. Too much thatch can lead to pest infestation and disease. To reduce thatch, gently rake the lawn or topdress with a thin layer of organic matter or gypsum, then water.

OVERFERTILIZE

Overfertilization promotes the development of thatch, can induce fungal growth, and stresses the lawn. Generally, lawns should be fertilized once in early fall (the most important) and in early spring. The timing and number of applications may vary depending on the local climate and soil conditions.

Just Water

by Roger B. Swain

My grandfather left me his taste for horseradish, for buttermilk, and for raw oysters. These fit me well. What I have only recently grown into is his taste for water. His first stop when he came to visit was always the kitchen sink, where he would pour himself a glass of water—plain water in a plain glass—drink it down, and tell us again how good it was. We knew it came from a distinguished source, the Quabbin Reservoir in central Massachusetts. We had walked atop the aqueduct through which the water flows to Boston. But none of us could see any reason to be especially excited about the liquid itself. It was just water, the stuff you drank when there wasn't any more milk.

Older now, and better traveled, I find myself standing in line, clutching my passport, waiting to be let back into the United States. In this cavernous waiting room, this legal no-man's land, the mood is subdued. All of us, whatever the colors of our passports, are forced to reflect for a moment on the meaning of liberty. For me, it has become first and foremost the freedom to drink the water. Though water may be tasteless, colorless, and odorless, in the words of Antoine de Saint-Exupéry, it is life itself.

I haven't been gone long, or far. But I am world-weary of Coca Cola, and I have brushed my teeth with spit. The road has converted me to the one true drink: water, pure water, water that is free of foul smells or bad taste; free of algae, bacteria, protozoans, or other microscopic pestilence. I understand now with perfect clarity my grandfather's pilgrimage to our kitchen sink.

A few weeks hence, when I have drunk my fill, I may be tempted to take tapwater for granted again. But the freedom to drink from the faucet must be as vigilantly guarded as any other. Attacks are reported almost daily. Sometimes the news is of a single disaster, a tractor-trailer load of industrial chemicals spilling into a reservoir. But more often the encroachment is gradual, insidious. First the water begins to taste funny, but the health department assures the residents that it is safe to drink. Then people start to get sick. Investigations are begun, fingers are pointed, blame is assigned and denied. The water goes on tasting bad, and people are afraid to drink it.

Water purity is terribly fragile. Like minnows in a lake, contaminants spread quickly in the water, making it all but impossible to retrieve them once they are released. Entire well fields have had to be abandoned when they were salted by the runoff from nearby highways. The chemicals oozing into the earth from waste dumps can poison entire aquifers. In this country, just like in every other one, you have to watch what you drink.

This is a somewhat sobering thought for a citizen who is waiting to come home to his first real drink. So, too, is the realization that it is not enough to worry about the water flowing from our faucets. We must also think about the water above and below us. Every species on earth depends on water, not just our own. To allow it to become polluted simply because we are not at the moment thirsty is both shortsighted and selfish. Unless we are more careful, hikers will contaminate every mountain stream, our city effluent will foul every estuary. Fortunately, the task is as beautiful as it is important. Inspiration lies everywhere, in dewdrops and misty lakes, in marshes and tidepools.

It is my turn. I have come to the head of the line. I hold out my passport with its deep blue binding. The silver eagle ripples. The immigration officer smiles. I smile, too, and step forward, toward liberty and water for all.

The Facts About Water

from the Environmental Protection Agency

It's True!

- Of all the earth's water, 97 percent is ocean or sea.

- Only 1 percent of the earth's water is suitable for drinking.

- Water you drink may have been part of the dinosaur era.

- Water regulates the earth's temperature. It is a natural insulator.

- Water is the only substance found on earth naturally in three forms: solid, liquid, and gas.

- A birch tree gives off 70 gallons per day in evaporation.

- 95 percent of a tomato, 80 percent of an ear of corn, 70 percent of an elephant is water.

- It takes 9.3 gallons of water to process one can of fruit or vegetables.

- It takes 1,500 gallons of water to process one barrel of beer.

- It takes 33,100 gallons of water to process one ton of beet sugar to make processed sugar.

- Each adult in the United States uses an average of 125 to 150 gallons a day, an estimated 40 percent more water than is necessary.

- Over the past few years an estimated 2.3 trillion gallons of inadequately treated sewage were dumped into U.S. coastal waters.

You can help!

In every room . . .
- Repair leaky water faucets, indoors and out. One leaky faucet can use up to 4,000 gallons of water per month.

- Install faucet aerators. These inexpensive devices can reduce water use up to 60 percent, while maintaining a strong flow.

In the kitchen . . .
- Save 10 to 15 gallons by peeling and cleaning vegetables in a large bowl instead of under the running tap.

- When handwashing dishes, save 15 gallons by soaking dirty dishes in the basin, then rinsing them off.

- Run fully loaded dishwashers to save 15 gallons per load and hot-water costs, too.

- When buying a new dishwasher, select one with a "light wash" option. Newer models use 20 percent less water than older ones.

In the bathroom . . .
- Take short showers instead of baths. Showers use an average of 5 to 7 gallons per minute, three times less than the water used to take a bath. A low-flow showerhead (still provides a good flow!) will cut water use to 3 gallons per minute.

- Shut the water off when you brush your teeth, shave, or soap in the shower. This will save 4 gallons when brushing your teeth and 9 gallons when shaving.

- A toilet displacement device (check at your hardware store) can save 5 to 7 gallons per flush. When buying a new toilet, select a low-flush model; it uses only 1½ gallons per flush.

On wash day . . .
- Run only full loads!

- When you need a new machine, buy a water-saving model that can be adjusted to load size and has a suds-saving option. New models use 40 percent less water than older models.

In your yard . . .
- Plant indigenous species suited to your area, which can survive on as much as 54 percent less water than nonnative plants outdoor plants. Ask your local nursery for plant and grass species that require less water.

- Mow your lawn with water retention in mind. Set mower blades on a high setting (2- to 3-inch grass length as opposed to golf-course-short) to provide natural ground shade and to promote water retention by the soil.

- Water your lawn and garden in the morning when evaporation is lowest.

- Water no more that 1 inch per week, applied slowly to prevent runoff. Place several empty cans around the yard when watering to determine how long it takes to supply 1 inch of water.

- Collect rainwater for watering plants using a barrel covered with a screen.

- When washing your car, turn off the hose between rinses to save up to 150 gallons per washing.

- "Dry-clean" decks and driveways with a broom instead of a hose.

The Invasion of the Asphalt Snatchers

by Eric Swanson

The Egyptians did it. So did the Assyrians. The Babylonians did it on a very grand scale, and theirs became one of the Seven Wonders of the Ancient World. The Greeks, being Greek, did it for a reason; the Romans, being Roman, did it sheerly for pleasure. The Arabs did it around water, the Indians did it with flowers and fruit trees, and the Japanese, in doing it, exercised characteristic restraint. Just about anywhere large groups of people have come together in permanent settlements, someone came up with the idea of building a park.

Throughout history and across cultures, parks and plantings have performed a vital function in the lives of cities and city dwellers. Oases in the middle of stone deserts, parks and other green areas have helped dissolve the isolation and stress that tend to develop among people who live in cities, promoting a sense of community more readily experienced in rural or suburban areas. Tensions fade during a stroll through a shady wooded path; spirits rise on fragrant clouds of wisteria or jasmine. Many parks sponsor musical, theatrical, and other cultural events, where urbanites can share a common diversion. Some parks enclose small zoos, where denizens of the asphalt jungle can commune for a while with more congenial species. Meanwhile, trees and other plantings provide substantial health benefits, cooling hot city air, trapping harmful pollutants, and reducing noise levels along busy highways and byways.

Public gardens flourished in Europe for centuries before Americans understood their value. In 1853 New York City dedicated approximately 800 acres of land in the center of Manhattan for use as a public park. After several years of wrangling over plans, the city's commissioners decided to sponsor a landscape design contest, awarding the prize to Frederick Law Olmsted and Calvert Vaux. Through a number of innovations, which included sinking crosstown roads below the parks surface and providing a number of access routes for smaller vehicles through the park itself, Olmsted and Vaux demonstrated that municipal park design could successfully integrate practical details and aesthetic excellence. The city councilmen, naturally, congratulated themselves on their foresight and took no end of pleasure in pointing out that they were the first to carry out so vast a public landscape project. Not to be outdone, municipal planners across the country undertook to create their own parks, and a national public landscaping movement began, the lasting benefit of which can be felt on any sizzling summer afternoon.

Since the heady days of late-19th- and early-20th-century pub-lic works, the pace of urban park spending has slowed somewhat, and private organizations have sprung up across the country to fill the gap. The Lila Wallace Reader's Digest Urban Parks Institute, for example, funds a national effort to create new parks in underserved neighborhoods, to restore failing parks, and to promote the use of parks for cultural activities, children's school workshops, job training programs, and community activism. Project for Public Spaces, Inc., meanwhile, has designed and managed public areas in over 600 communities since 1975, using techniques such as time-lapse filming and community surveys to analyze how people use public areas.

Despite crowding, development, and the decay of once vital cores, cities across the country have managed to hold fast the dream of green against the onslaught of asphalt philistines. Today New York City's Department of Parks & Recreation manages more than 27,000 acres throughout the five boroughs, including 1,500 parks, zoos, forests, and botanical gardens, and nearly 600,000 street plantings; recently, the department has restored more than 5,000 acres of

New York City's natural woodlands and wetlands, recovered more than $40 million in damages from major pollution claims, and acquired more than 500 acres of new parkland. Kansas City, Missouri, maintains approximately 200 parks and more than 130 miles of boulevards and parkways covering more than 10,000 acres. Down California way, San Diego is home to some 14,000 acres of public green, including the magnificent 1,400-acre Balboa Park in the city's historic district, a 4,600-acre site along Mission Bay, a 52-mile scenic drive, and Anza Borrego State Park, which at 6,000 acres constitutes the largest state park in the 48 contiguous states. Seattle's parks were originally designed way back when by Frederick Law Olmsted's company, and although the entire plan was never fully executed, the city boasts nearly 400 public parks and nature trails covering approximately 6,200 acres.

Florida's byzantine sprawl of cities known as Greater Metropolitan Miami encompasses the nation's sixth-largest park system, with 13,000 of parkland managed by Dade County, an additional 500 acres managed by the state, and upwards of 70 smaller sites maintained by the cities themselves.

Clearly, one doesn't have to be a Hottentot to enjoy some green when the sun gets hot. Although we Americans don't have public baths like the Romans or sacred groves like the Greeks, we have, in our own fashion, come to appreciate the benefits afforded by parks and other public green areas. Without them, our nation's cities would wither—physically, culturally, and spiritually. Like green shoots that push their way through cracks in the asphalt, urban parks remind us that, no matter how grown up we think we are, we will never be as wise or love so well as our common Mother Nature.

R ECYCLING

by Roger B. Swain

Listen to the voice of a tropical forest. Not to the raucous duet of parrots, or the buzz of hovering flies, or even the love-struck chorus of frogs. Listen instead to the harmony of the falling leaves, twigs, bits of bark and fruit, the periodic crash of a large limb. Some of what falls has been intentionally shed by plants, some has been spilled by animals feeding in the canopy, some is the result of catastrophe—a branch so overloaded with ferns, moss, bromeliads, and other epiphytes that it collapses under the weight of excess vegetation.

From the sound of the forest, the ground beneath it should be deep in debris. Yet despite the steady rain of organic matter, little ever accumulates. No spongy layer of humus-rich topsoil cushions the visitor's step. To a traveler familiar with northern woodlands, with groves of oaks and aspen and pines, the soil underfoot is inexplicably bare.

What happens to all the litter? It gets reused. In the temperate zone, fallen organic matter can lie intact on the ground for years. In the tropics, it seldom lasts more than a few weeks or months. Termites, fungi, and bacteria, working in the comfort of heat and humidity, swarm over any fallen leaf or twig and set about dismantling it. Soon, thanks to the partnership of fungi and the roots of tropical vegetation, the essential nutrients that might otherwise have been washed away by rain are safely back in the forest's living tissues.

It is easy to look at the luxuriance of a tropical forest—the palms and lianas, the flowering tree trunks and plank buttresses, leaves so dense they blot out the sun—and assume that the soil beneath it all must be especially rich. But the appearance is deceiving. The original fertility of many tropical soils is long gone, stripped away by millions of years of slowly percolating rainwater. That the land is nevertheless occupied by the grandest and most complex community on earth is a monument to what can be done with strict adherence to the principle of recycling.

Those of us who reside in temperate latitudes, who are more familiar with fireweed than with flame-of-the-forest, are only just beginning to know the tropics. Having been born into a land of plenty, we are still beginners at the fine art of conservation. We have been plowing through the legacy of the last Ice Age, young soil that still retains most of its original fertility. Our civilization depends on an annual harvest of grains and grasses. Yet we have been so careless with the soil's fertility that much of it has been lost. Even today, in towns and cities, we rake up the leaves that fall from the trees and bury them in plastic bags. When the nutrients from these graves surface again, they come back so contaminated they haunt us.

Our way of life is threatening our survival, and the survival of what little temperate wilderness remains. Because the next Ice Age is too far off to rescue us in time, we ought to start economizing. But making do with less is such a bleak prospect that few of us are eager to begin. That is what makes the tropics so attractive, not just to first-time visitors but even more to those who have spent time there. Here is an example of recycling that makes our own fledgling efforts seem pitiful. Here is a fantastically complicated, enormously sophisticated world constructed entirely from used components. Even the most accomplished tropical biologists consider themselves neophytes. But if an overriding wisdom is emerging from our preliminary studies in tropical forests, it is that salvage and salvation have the same roots.

Migratory Songbirds: The Ties That Bind Us

by Lisa J. Petit and
Daniel R. Petit

Quick, what comes to mind when you think of the tropics? Sandy beaches and swaying palms? Perhaps a dim and steamy jungle, alive with the sounds of exotic birds and other unusual creatures? Most of us in North America think of tropical countries as faraway places, with which we have little in common. But there is a direct connection between our backyards and the tropics. Each spring and fall, millions of small songbirds migrate the great distances between the two regions.

Nearly half of all bird species found in North America are Neotropical migratory birds, so named because they migrate to the New World (Neo) tropics, which comprise Mexico, Central and South America, and the Caribbean. These migrants include many hawks, ducks, geese, and the majority of shorebirds and songbirds.

Migratory songbirds make the long and perilous trip to North America to take advantage of the great abundance of nutritious insects needed to raise their young. They have colorful and poetic names like Wood Thrush, Scarlet Tanager, and Bobolink and include nearly all of the warblers, vireos, flycatchers, orioles, and other species that depend on the insects that disappear during cold northern winters.

These songbirds abdicate their northern habitat each winter, but they return each spring to our woodlands, marshes, fields, and grasslands, bringing their beautiful songs to warm our souls. We may think of them as "our" birds, living here and spending the winter in warmer climates, but in fact migratory songbirds spend most of their time in the tropics.

In the tropics, migratory songbirds live in a variety of habitats. As long as there is enough food for their own survival, they are fairly flexible in where they can live because they are not saddled with trying to find a place to nest and raise their young, However, these birds have fewer and fewer places to go.

Throughout their journey, in tropical and northern areas alike, migratory songbirds face perils and pitfalls that are mostly the result of their habitat shrinking or deteriorating in quality. Tropical forests and woodlands, which are particularly important for many migrants, are being cleared for cattle pasture and large-scale agriculture and development.

Some tropical "human" habitats such as plantations of coffee grown under a canopy of shade trees, groves of citrus trees, and residential areas with an abundance of fruiting and flowering trees can be good homes. However, the cutting of shade trees on coffee plantations to increase yields and the use of pesticides in citrus groves threaten these oases.

Just as on your family vacation you rely on gas stations and hotels to help you along the way, migratory birds rely on our woodlots, neighborhood parks, and shady backyards to find the fuel, rest, and protection they need to travel thousands of miles twice a year. If we want the songbirds to keep coming back to us each year, we must make certain that their five-star hotels don't all change to seedy motels and that their habitats aren't bulldozed and paved.

We must realize our importance in the cycle of these small travelers and recognize that we share the responsibility for their survival with the people of the tropics. So, with your next sip of coffee or bite of an orange, think of the Tennessee Warbler or Baltimore Oriole that may have been perched where those plants grew, perhaps in Mexico, Belize, or Panama. As you watch your daffodils herald the spring or plant your bulbs in the fall, think of the millions of tiny travelers winging over your head in search of the next rest stop, the next gas station—perhaps in your very own yard!

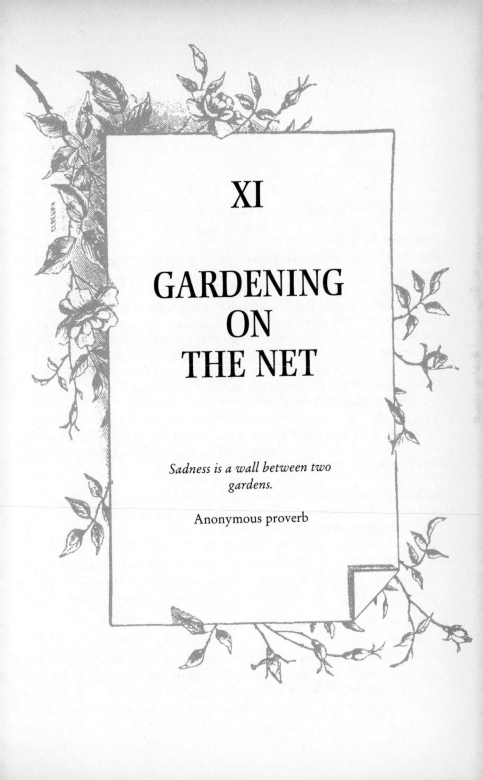

XI

GARDENING
ON
THE NET

*Sadness is a wall between two
gardens.*

Anonymous proverb

A Web of Gardens

by Adele Q. Brown

Blackwell's Gardening Books is a bookstore in the United Kingdom providing "search and find" books on gardening subjects. Naturally, you can order from them as well.
http://www.blackwell.co.uk/bookshops/oxtour/shelfcats/gardening.html

Garden Web provides links by country, states, regions, or subject area. The thorough list of sites includes plant databases (e.g., "medicinal plants of Native America"), horticulture sites, Cooperative Extension Services,botanical gardens and museums, societies and associations, publishing links, directories of nurseries and catalogs, and a search component for anything you did not find in the extensive lists above.
http://www.gardenweb.com/v1/

Gardening Suppliers Index connects you to over 20 catalog lists on the Net from Gardener's Eden to Snow Pond Farm to The Worm Factory.
http://www.cog.brown.edu/gardening/f33idx.html

Gardening.com provides essential information about gardening via a plant encyclopedia, yellow pages, magazine rack, and garden locales.
http://gardening.com/

GardenNet claims to be "the premier garden center on the Internet." It is a classy site with an on-line magazine, *The Ardent Gardener*; a visitor's center; book review file; flower show schedule; and garden literature review.
http://www.trine.com/GardenNet/home.htm

Internet Directory for Botany—Gardening is a superb, alphabetical listing by subject (e.g., "african violet") of international web links.
http://www.helsinki.fi/kmus/bothort.html

Joe and Mindy's Oklahoma Gardening Page sounds folksy, but it's chock full of incredible information maintained by two completely overworked graduate students. If you go to their main Home page, http://www.nhn.uoknor.edu/~howard/howard.html, you'll get information on astrophysics, astronomy, science fiction, and gardening. Their Gardening site has a virtual library, book reviews, garden catalog links, the Royal Botanic Gardens, and plenty more.
http://www.nhn.uoknor.edu/~howard/garden.html

Mailing List for Gardeners connects people by topics to lists that may be of interest to the specialized gardener.
http://www.prairienet.org/garden-gate/maillist.htm

Noah's Ark Organic Farmer provides the most up-to-date information about organic gardening and links to other organic gardening resources.
http://rain.org:80/~sals/my.html

Shawn's Garden Pathfinder is a great spot for a quick answer. This web page is made up solely of links to other sites, which include the U.S. Department of Agriculture for their hardiness chart; horticulture guides; an encyclopedia; a glossary; specialty magazines; and addresses for gardening societies.
http://gopher.libraries.wayne.edu/LISP/garden.html

The Garden Gate on the Prairienet is full of wonderful information and links to other websites. It's a great place to start a tour.
http://www.prairienet.org/garden-gate/

The Neighborhood's Gardening Launch Pad is a terrific spot that contains over 1,300 links in 42 categories. Click on a category such as "orchids," "herbs," "ponds," or "garden tours" and you're connected.
http://www.tpoint.net/neighbor/

Weekend Gardener™ is a weekly electronic guide with the tag line "practical horticulture for busy people." The user-friendly, upscale site provides a free weekly magazine; website links; weather lore; daily garden tips; and more. Sign up at the visitor's center to receive additional gardening tidbits for free.
http://www.chestnut-sw.com/weekend.htm

Weather On the Web

by Adele Q. Brown

Historical Tornado Data is a Storm Prediction Center (SPC) site maintained by the University of Oklahoma at Norman in the heart of tornado country. The site contains as much information about these terrifying twisters as any one person absorb.
http://www.nssl.uoknor.edu/~spc/archive/tornadoes/

Purdue University's Hurricane Archives provide the quintessential information about tropical cyclones in the Atlantic and Pacific Basin going back to the 19th century. The data are provided in various chart formats, the best of which is a cartographic tracking by year of all Atlantic Coast tropical storms and hurricanes. For the devout only.
http://wxp.atms.purdue.edu/hurricane.html

The National Oceanic and Atmospheric Administration (NOAA) is a site run by an agency of the U.S. Department of Commerce. You will find links to the National Weather Service (NWS), the Climate Prediction Center (CPC), the Marine Prediction Center (MPC), the Aviation Weather Center (AWC), the Tropical Prediction Center (TPC), the Storm Prediction Center (SPC), and the National Center for Environmental Prediction (NCEP). All of these bureaus have specialized responsibilities in weather-data collection and analysis.
http://www.awc-kc.noaa.gov/other-web.html

- **The National Weather Service (NWS)**, perhaps the best-known NOAA agency, is the most likely stop on a weather tour. This site provides files on current weather, climate and historical data, and weather topics, as well as containing a search feature for more-specific data.
  http://www.nws.noaa.gov

- **The National Climatic Data Center (NCDC)** is another NOAA agency that provides information on products, publications, and services, including data on past weather events such as the 25 deadliest tornadoes and a listing by state of tornadoes in the last 50 years. **http://www.ncdc.noaa.gov**

- **The Storm Prediction Center (SPC)** maintains on-line data files and is also part of the NOAA. You can access the archives, severe storm statistics, forecast products, and publications. **http://.whirlwind100.nssl.uoknor.edu/~spc/**

The Weather Channel maintains a full-service Internet site that is more graphically oriented and fancier, but slower, than some of the other sites. You can search weather by state, find a business traveler's forecast, check out ski or sailing conditions, and sign up to get weather delivered directly to your mailbox.
http://www.weather.com/

USA TODAY Weather Almanac On Line is a terrific site if you need to find that fast fact about weather averages, the time of sunrises and moonrises, and weather records.
http://www.usatoday.com/weather/walm0.htm

USA TODAY's Ask Jack is a site where columnist Jack Williams responds to weather questions submitted by readers. These columns are sorted by subject matter and can provide more-detailed information than the general index. Links to other Internet sites are a welcome addition for the serious student.
http://web.usatoday.com/weather/askjack/wjack5.html

USA TODAY's Weather Index provides one of the most thorough weather archives on-line. Easy to use and access, the index can be searched by letter or subject. A click to "H" and the diverse topics range from "hail" to "heat bursts" to "hydrology."
http://www.usatoday.com/weather/windex.htm

About the Authors

Ingrid Abramovitch lives in New York City, where she writes about culture and lifestyle.

Tom Armstrong is director emeritus of the Whitney Museum of American Art.

Barbara Ashmun, author of *The Garden Design Primer* and *200 Tips for Growing Flowers in the Pacific Northwest*, teaches, consults, and gardens in Portland, Oregon.

Adele Q. Brown is content to be based in New York City, where she safely writes about disasters elsewhere.

A. Wayne Cahilly is the manager of the arboretum and grounds at the New York Botanical Garden and a home gardener in northern New Jersey.

Thomas C. Cooper is the editor of *Horticulture* magazine and the author of *Odd Lots*.

Paula Deitz is a cultural critic in the fields of art, architecture and landscape design. She is coeditor of *The Hudson Review* and writes regularly for the *New York Times, Gardens Illustrated* and other magazines here and abroad.

Dr. Ernest T. DeMarie III is the curator of Desert and Subtropical Plants at the New York Botanical Garden.

Virginia Devlin is communications manager for All-America Rose Selections and a budding rose gardener in Chicago.

Page Dickey is the author of *Breaking Ground: Portraits of Ten Garden Designers* and *Duck Hill Journal: A Year in a Country Garden* and has been a regular contributor to *House & Garden, House Beautiful,* and *Elle Decor.*

Susan Dooley writes about gardens and lives in Maine.

Ken Druse, author, photographer, environmentalist, and gardener, has chronicled the development of a distinctly American gardening style in his books, such as *The Natural Garden* (1989), *The Natural Habitat Garden* (1994), and *The Collector's Garden* (1996), published by Clarkson Potter, New York.

Nicolas H. Ekstrom, a landscape designer and horticultural consultant and a director of The Horticultural Society of New York, is coauthor of *Perennials for American Gardens.*

Stephanie Flack is NatureServe project manager for The Nature Conservancy in Arlington, Virginia.

Charlotte M. Frieze, the author of *The Zone Garden* series and *Social Gardens,* is a landscape architect with Robert A. M. Stern Architects.

Daiva K. Gasperetti designs dried flower arrangements for her company, Belles Fleurs de Daiva, in New York City.

Jeffrey Glassberg is president of the North American Butterfly Association (NABA), a nonprofit group working to promote the public enjoyment and conservation of butterflies.

Marlene Goddu is the chef and proprietor, with her husband, Marc, of the Mattapoisett Inn in southeastern Massachusetts, the oldest seaside inn in the country still operating in its original structure.

Wendy Gordon is cofounder and executive director of Mothers & Others for a Livable Planet, an environmental education organization working to promote consumer choices that are safe and sustainable for current and future generations.

Jan Hack lives and cooks in Ann Arbor, Michigan, with her husband and three children.

Elizabeth L. Haskins, lives in New York City with her husband and son. She tends a garden in South Salem, New York.

Peter C. Jones is the author of *The Changing Face of America* and the coauthor, with Lisa MacDonald, of *Hero Dogs*.

Daniel R. Petit is a wildlife biologist with the U.S. Fish and Wildlife Service, Office of Migratory Bird Management.

Lisa J. Petit is a research wildlife biologist at the Smithsonian Migratory Bird Center.

Anne Raver is author of *Deep in the Green* and writes about gardening and the environment for the *New York Times*.

Megan Grey Rollins is a freelance natural history illustrator, whose work has appeared in numerous publications in the evironmental community. She lives in Richmond, Virginia.

Marty Ross writes the monthly gardening column for Universal Press Syndicate; she is also the weekly gardening columnist for the *Kansas City Star* and writes for several national gardening magazines.

Michael Ruggiero is senior curator of the New York Botanical Garden and author of *The American Garden Guide: Perennial Gardening*; *The Serious Gardener Series: Reliable Roses* and other works.

Felder Rushing, author of *Passalong Plants* and *Gardening, Southern Style*, is an eighth-generation southern gardener.

Nina Straus, a Sagittarius, is the author of *Dostoyevsky and the Woman Question*. She teaches at Purchase College, SUNY.

Roger B. Swain is the science editor of *Horticulture* magazine, the host of *The Victory Garden* on PBS-TV, and the author of numerous books.

Eric Swanson is the author of *We're Having a Kitten* and *We're Having a Puppy* as well as numerous magazine articles.

Emma Sweeney is the author of *The Complete Idiot's Guide to Gardening*. She is working toward her Commercial Horticulture Certificate at the New York Botanical Garden.

ACKNOWLEDGMENTS

The editors wish to express their profound appreciation to the authors who contributed to *The Gardener's Almanac;* to Frances Tenenbaum for her generous advice and unwavering support; to Adele Q. Brown, who plowed the fertile ground of the Internet with insight and endless good humor; to Nancy Stabile for her flawless copyediting; to their friend and colleague Doris Straus for her inspired, original design; and to their partner Roger Straus III, without whom this project never would have happened.